FAT[...] an[...] THE GREAT CONSPIRACY

by
Deirdre Manifold

With 3 Sections Added In This 1993 Edition

**Our Lady's Urgent Appeal
to Us in the 1990's**

**Our Lady of Fatima's Most
Important Request**

**The Plans of Christ the King
for True World Peace**

Published by:
The Militia of Our Immaculate Mother
Box 602 Fort Erie, Ontario L2A 5X3
85 Allen Street, Suite 505, Buffalo, NY 14202

Printed in U.S.A.

PUBLISHER'S PREFACE FOR THE 1992 EDITION

Pope John Paul II at Fatima on May 13, 1991 prophetically stated. . . "there exists the danger that Marxism will be replaced by another form of Atheism". That is what we now see taking place before our eyes in the latter half of 1991, with the staged coup in Russia on August 19, 1991, and with the "resignation" of Gorbachev in December, 1991.

To understand these events and to appreciate what is really happening in the world, we need to know about many forces which have been dominant in forming the steps of the current political scene both domestically and internationally.

This book, *Fatima And The Great Conspiracy*, does not content itself giving us a shallow analysis based on yesterday's events, but looks back into history to trace more completely the real, dark forces of atheism and satanism that have planned to take control.

We must not be deceived by the very anti-God forces which control many of the positions of influence and power in our own countries today. This too is part of their program. We must not be tricked into thinking in terms of right or left, liberal or conservative, etc., as these terms are redefined as it suits our enemies' purposes in order to deceive us.

We must rather think in terms of truth or falsehood, right or wrong, good or bad. We must look at world events and domestic politics as Jesus Christ and His Mother would have us look at them. Then and only then can we become part of the solution and not part of the problem.

The world is in great crisis, a terrible crisis, and Our Lord and Our Lady want you to do your part on the side of God and Christ the King. Your help is urgently needed. But first you must be more fully informed. This book lays the ground work for that purpose.

In the first and longest section we are given the background to the great conspiracy against God and man. It brings us up to the present time. It also touches upon Our Lady of Fatima's plan for true and lasting peace, the only one that will work.

The second section, "Our Lady's Urgent Appeal," explains more fully the conspiracy in theological terms, and the fact that Our Lady of Fatima is the only answer to the crisis in both the short and long term.

The fourth section points out what are the real goals of the enemies of Christ, and they are contrasted with the real aims of Christ the King for society, families, governments and economic groups. Satan, Christ's enemy and our enemy, has succeeded in deceiving even pious Christians into serving satan's interests because he has hidden his real agenda from them.

The fourth section makes it clear what satan's aims are, and helps us see through the various camouflages - be it labelled liberal, conservative, right or left, communist, soviet, nationalist or democratic.

We urge you to read this book in its entirety and join Our Lord and His Holy Mother Mary, Our Lady of Fatima, in the final battle which will end in victory when Her Full Fatima Message is heard, understood, loved and obeyed. Much depends on you. Please listen to Their voices today. God bless you and Our Lady keep you ever close to Her Divine Son Jesus.

Contents

Publisher's Preface for 1992 Edition i
Table of Contents iii

**Section I - Fatima and the
          Great Conspiracy** 1
Author's Preface 3
Chapter 1
The Message of Fatima 7
Chapter 2
The Roots of Communism 19
Chapter 3
Money — The Root of All Evil 43
Chapter 4
The Role Of Secret Societies 69
Chapter 5
The Essence of Communism 81
Chapter 6
The Takeover In Russia 93
Chapter 7
Living Under Communism 105
Chapter 8
Handing China Over to the Communists . . . 119
Chapter 9
Is Peace Possible? 153
Postscript 175

**Section II - Our Lady's Urgent Appeal
          to Us** 177
Introduction to Section II 179

Part I
We Must Choose Now **181**
Part II
Outline of the Crisis **185**
Chapter 1 **Our Rights Comes From God** **186**
Chapter 2 **Our God Given Rights**
                         Openly Attacked **190**
Part III
Cause For Hope - Our Lady **197**
Part IV
What You Can Do **207**

Section III - Our Lady of Fatima's Most
                    Important Request **215**

Section IV - The Plans of Christ the King
                    for True World Peace,
                    Contrasted Against the Plans
                    of Satan for World Tyranny
                    and Destruction **221**
Introduction to Section IV **223**
The Programme Of Christ
vs. Satan's Plans **227**
First Point
The Role of the Catholic Church **227**
Second Point
Relationship of States to the
Catholic Church **232**
Third Point
Christian Family Life **236**

Fourth Point
Christian Education 240
Fifth Point
Widespread Ownership
of Private Property 244
Sixth Point
The Monetary System: Servant
or Slave Master 248
Seventh Point
The Role of Supernatural Grace in the Public
Life of Society 253
A Further Point
The Right to Life 260

Section V - Bibliographies 261
   Short Bibliography to Section I 263
   Short Bibliography to Section II And III . . . 267
   Short Bibliography to Section IV 268

Appendix 269

Section I

Fatima and the
Great Conspiracy

by
Deirdre Manifold

FATIMA
AND
THE GREAT CONSPIRACY

by
Deirdre Manifold

Originally Published by
FIRINNE PUBLICATIONS
Galway, Ireland

1st Edition - October 1982
2nd Edition - December 1982
3rd Edition - March 1983
4th Edition - February 1984
5th Edition - February 1985
6th Edition - May 1987
7th Edition - September 1992
8th Edition - July 1993

AUTHOR'S PREFACE

On New Year's Day, 1982, a friend and I were discussing the awful state of the world and why this era should seem to be like no other era in history. I asked him:

"Do you accept the accidental theory of history, or do you believe in the Insider-Conspiratorial theory of history?"

He looked at me and said: "What exactly do you mean by the accidental theory of history or the Conspiratorial theory of history?"

My reply was something like this:

"Do you really believe that everything that has happened, in this century say, has happened by accident, say for instance the two great wars, the depression in between, all the local no-win wars ever since, and now the massive unemployment and the frightening inflation rate, do you really believe that mankind has no control over them, that like earthquakes they just happen and we have to make the best of them?"

His reply to that was, "I'm afraid I never seriously gave it much thought, I just accept what the newspapers say."

Then I asked him if he had ever heard what Disraeli had said that the world was ruled by very different people from what was imagined by those who were not behind the lines (scenes), much later Roosevelt was to say that whenever anything happened in politics you may bet it was planned that way.

Then I went on to tell him that for a long time scholars had ignored as a serious subject for study what went on behind the scenes, but the events of this century, being like no other period in time, made them curious. They began to delve behind the scenes, to root out the evidence, and have now made the unchallengeable case that the world is ruled by a handful of men who can bring on wars, depressions, unemployment, inflation, anything they want.

My friend looked incredulous and naturally being a good man asked why anybody, or any body of men, would want to do such awful things. He then said who are these mysterious men you talk about and why should they want to bring so much suffering into the world?

"They are the world's richest men, and their object is power."

"I find that very hard to believe."

"Fair enough, but do you believe that a man called Hitler once lived, that he wanted power and succeeded in getting an awful lot of it."

"Yes, that is a fact of history."

"As it happened, Hitler was a fool. He sat down and wrote down everything he intended to do. Now if Hitler were really clever he would have plotted in secret and taken the world by surprise, as the scholars have now proved the Insider/Conspirators have always done. How they must have rubbed their hands in glee when they read Hitler's *Mein Kampf* and said to themselves: this is our puppet par excellence. He

4

is made to order, all we need to do is set him up, finance him, keep other countries weak until he is ready to go to war. Nothing will help our plans for total world dictatorship like a good hot war, where we will control both sides as we have always done. Just now the peoples of the world are so sick of war it will take a Hitler to force them into it. In whatever way they said or thought this to themselves this is exactly what they did. This is the subject matter of Professor Anthony Sutton's book *Wall Street and the Rise of Hitler,* which, it has been said, makes every previous book on World War II obsolete. Oh, I'm sure you never heard of it. Books which tell too much of the truth get the silent treatment."

"Yes, but you haven't said who they are or how they acquired such power. What kind of tricks did they pull off to give them such power?"

"Despotic power had its roots in the Reformation, but after that there were two great turning points in history, namely the foundation of the Bank of England and the founding of a group known as the Illuminati by one Adam Weishaupt in Bavaria in 1776. The former by sleight of hand got control of the coin of the realm into private hands for the first time in history and the latter used that control and all disparate revolutionary groups for the one purpose of total world slavery."

"I still find that very hard to believe."

"You don't accept something so awful because you haven't read the evidence. Would you know the Greek language if you had never studied Greek?"

"No."

"Did you ever hear of the Message of Fatima, you may think it has nothing to do with what we are

5

talking about, but it is very relevant?"

"Yes, but only in a vague way, I'd need to know more."

"Well, in 1917, when Communism was but a word, the meaning of which very few people knew, Our Lady appeared to three small children at Fatima in Portugal. There She told them during a number of visits everything that has happened in the world from that time up to this day. She appealed for prayers and penance and sacrifice by the faithful. Otherwise She said Russia would spread her errors throughout the world, many nations would be lost, and the Holy Father would have much to suffer."

"I have to agree all that has already happened, but go on . . ."

Chapter 1

THE MESSAGE OF FATIMA

The story of Fatima begins in 1915 when three children, Lucia Santos, aged 8, and her two companions, noticed a peculiar cloud in the sky. It appeared on three different occasions, more than ordinarily white and perfectly visible as a human form. It was a foretaste of what was to come.

Apparitions of the Angel

1. In the spring of 1916 it came again, "a light whiter than snow, revealing the form of a young man. He spoke: "Fear not, I am the Angel of Peace. Pray with me." Kneeling down he bowed his head to the ground and prayed, ending by telling the children they should pray thus: "My God, I believe, I adore, I hope, and I love You. I ask pardon for those who do not believe, nor adore, nor hope, nor love You." He then said, "The Hearts of Jesus and Mary are attentive to the voice of your supplication." He then disappeared.

2. In mid-summer, 1916, the Angel appeared again quite suddenly saying: "What are you doing? Pray, pray a great deal. The Hearts of Jesus and Mary have designs of mercy on you. Offer up prayers and sacrifices to the Most High. Make everything you do a sacrifice, and offer it as an act of reparation for the

sins by which He is offended, and in supplication for the conversion of sinners. Bring peace to your country in this way. I am the Guardian Angel of Portugal. Above all, accept and bear with submission the sufferings sent you by the Lord."

3. In the autumn of 1916 the Angel appeared a third time, holding in his hand a Chalice, surmounted by a Host, from which drops of blood were falling into the Chalice. Leaving the Chalice and Host suspended in the air, he prostrated on the ground and repeated this prayer three times: "Most Holy Trinity, Father, Son and Holy Spirit, I adore You profoundly, I offer You the most precious Body, Blood, Soul and Divinity of Our Lord Jesus Christ, present in all the Tabernacles of the world in reparation for all the outrages, sacrileges and indifferences by which He is offended. By the infinite merits of His Most Sacred Heart, through the intercession of the Immaculate Heart of Mary, I beg for the conversion of poor sinners". Then rising, the Angel took the Chalice and the Host. He gave the Host to Lucia, and the contents of the Chalice to Jacinta and Francisco, saying: "Take and drink the Body and Blood of Jesus Christ, horribly outraged by ungrateful men. Repair their crimes and console your God."

Apparitions of Our Lady

1. On May 13th, 1917, Lucia, Francisco and Jacinta were playing in the Cova da Iria, about a mile away from home, when suddenly they were startled by what appeared to be a flash of lightning. Then they saw a beautiful Lady dressed in white, poised over a

holm oak sapling. She was more brilliant than the sun, radiating a sparkling light. The Lady spoke: "Do not be afraid. I will do you no harm. I am from Heaven, and I have come to ask you to come here for six months on the 13th day at the same time. Later on I will tell you what I want and I will return here a seventh time."

Lucia addressed the Lady: "Shall I go to Heaven?" "Yes, you will." "And Jacinta?" "She will go also." "And Francisco?" "He will go there too, but he must say many Rosaries first."

Our Lady asked the children: "Do you wish to offer up to God all the sufferings He desires to send you in reparation for the sins by which He is offended, and in supplication for the conversion of sinners?" When the children replied: "Yes, we do." Our Lady said: "Then you will have much to suffer, but the grace of God will comfort you."

Finally Our Lady instructed the children: "Say the Rosary every day in order to obtain peace for the world and the end of the war."

2. June 13th, 1917. The three children had just finished saying the Rosary with a group of people when Our Lady appeared at the same spot again, and spoke with Lucia: "I want you to say the Rosary every day, and to learn to read. Later I will tell you what I want." "I will take Jacinta and Francisco to Heaven soon, but you must wait here for some time longer. Jesus wishes to make use of you to make Me known and loved. He wants to establish in the world devotion to My Immaculate Heart." Lucia was sad at the thought of being left alone without her cousins, but

Our Lady said to her: "Do not be disheartened. My Immaculate Heart will be your refuge, and the way that will lead you to God."

3. July 13th, 1917. Again there was a flash of light and Our Lady appeared over the holm oak and spoke with Lucia: "Continue to say the Rosary every day in honor of Our Lady in order to obtain peace for the world and the end of the war, because only She can obtain it." "I want You to tell us who You are and to perform a miracle so that everyone will believe that You appeared to us." said Lucia.

"Continue to come here every month. In October I will tell you who I am and what I want, and I will perform a miracle so that all may believe." "Sacrifice yourselves for sinners, and say often, especially when you make some sacrifice: 'Oh Jesus this is for the love of You, for the conversion of sinners, and in reparation for the sins committed against the Immaculate Heart of Mary.' "

Then the children were given a vision of Hell in which they could see demons and those who were damned. Our Lady said to them: "You have seen Hell where the souls of poor sinners go. In order to save them God wishes to establish in the world devotion to My Immaculate Heart. If you do what I tell you, many souls will be saved, and there will be peace. The war will end, but if men do not cease offending God another and more terrible war will break out during the reign of Pius XI (Remember he was not yet Pope) ... When you see a night lit up by an unknown light, know that that is the sign God gives you that He is about to punish the world for its crimes by means of war, hunger and persecution of the Church and the Holy Father. In order to prevent this, I shall come to ask for the consecration of Russia to My Immaculate Heart, and the Communion of Reparation of the First Saturdays. If My wishes are fulfilled, Russia will be converted and there will be peace. If not, *Russia will spread her errors throughout the world promoting wars and persecution of the Church.* The good will be martyred, the Holy Father will have much to suffer, and many nations will be annihilated, but in the end My Immaculate Heart will triumph. The Holy Father will consecrate Russia to Me and it will be converted, and a period of peace will be granted to the world . . . When you recite the Rosary, after each mystery say: 'Oh, my Jesus, forgive us our sins, save us from the fires of Hell. Lead all souls to Heaven, especially those who are most in need!' "

4. August 13th and 19th. On the morning of August 13th the three children were kidnapped by the hostile Government Administrator, and were thus prevented from being present in the Cova da Iria to meet Our Lady. In the meantime a crowd of about 18,000 had assembled there. At noon they heard a noise like thunder and saw a flash of light followed by a filmy cloud which came from the East and settled on the little holm oak, paused for a few moments, then rose and disappeared.

On August 19th the children returned home after their kidnapping experience and went out minding sheep at a place called Valinhos, a short distance from home. Here Our Lady appeared to them and spoke with Lucia: "I want you to continue going to the Cova da Iria on the 13th, and to continue saying the Rosary every day. In the last month I will perform a miracle so that all will believe." Then with a sad expression She said: "Pray, pray very much and make sacrifices for sinners, for many souls go to hell because they have nobody to pray and make sacrifices for them."

5. September 13th, 1917. As before there was a flash of light and Our Lady appeared on the holm oak and spoke with Lucia: "Continue to say the Rosary in order to obtain the end of the war. In October Our Lord will come, and also Our Lady of Dolours and Our Lady of (Mount) Carmel. St. Joseph will appear with the Child Jesus to bless the world. God is pleased with your sacrifices . . . In October I will perform a miracle so that all will believe."

6. October 13th, 1917. Each month from May to October people arrived in ever increasing numbers to be present for the apparition of Our Lady. On October 13th an estimated 70,000 were present in spite of torrential rain which began early on the evening of the 12th. At 12 o'clock Lucia announced that Our Lady was coming. There was a flash of light and Our Lady appeared on the holm oak, and spoke to Lucia: "I want to tell you that I wish a chapel to be erected here in My honor, for I am the Lady of the Rosary. Continue to say the Rosary every day, the war will soon end, and the soldiers will return to their homes . . . Do not offend God, Our Lord, any more, for He is already deeply offended."

As Our Lady disappeared, the curtain of clouds covering the whole sky split as if torn down the middle and rolled aside to leave the sun shining in a great expanse of sky. Although it was midday, the crowd could stare at the sun without being blinded, for it shone like a silver disc, very clear and bright but without the blazing dazzle of normal midday sun.

To the right of the sun the three children saw a vision of the Holy Family. St. Joseph and the Holy Child made the sign of the Cross three times over the crowd. Lucia then saw Our Lady of Dolours with Our Lord beside Her. He made the sign of the Cross over the crowd. Lucia then saw Our Lady of Mount Carmel with the Infant Jesus on Her knee.

The whole crowd then witnessed the miracle promised by Our Lady in Her earlier apparitions. As they gazed at the sun they saw it move. It began to spin like a giant wheel, shooting out great beams of colored light. Suddenly it seemed to break away from the sky, and moving in zig-zag jumps, appeared to plunge down towards the crowd. This phenomenon lasted about fifteen minutes and was witnessed not only by the huge crowd gathered in the Cova da Iria, but also by many people in the surrounding district up to thirty miles.

Apparitions Subsequent to 1917

When Francisco and Jacinta were very ill Our Lady came to tell them that She would come soon to take them to Heaven. Francisco died April 4th, 1919.

Jacinta was to go to two hospitals "Not to be cured but to suffer more for the conversion of sinners." Our Lady appeared to her and told her: "The sin which sends most people to perdition is the sin of the flesh; people should do without luxuries; they should not remain obstinate in their sins as they have done up to now; it is necessary to do much penance." On saying this Our Lady was very sad. Because of this Jacinta often exclaimed: "Oh, I am so sorry for Our Lady. I am so sorry for Her."

Jacinta went to Heaven on February 20th, 1920.

On December 10th, 1925, Our Lady with the Child Jesus appeared to Lucia at the Convent in Pontevedra where she was then a Dorothean Sister. Our Lady rested one hand on Lucia's shoulder, while in the other hand She held a Heart surrounded by sharp thorns. The Child Jesus spoke: "Have pity on the Heart of your Most Holy Mother: it is covered with thorns with which ungrateful men pierce it at every moment, and there is no one to remove them with an act of reparation." Then Our Lady said to Lucia: "My daughter, look at My Heart surrounded with the thorns with which ungrateful men pierce it at every moment by their blasphemies and ingratitude. You at least, try to console your Mother, and announce in My name that I promise to assist at the hour of death with all the graces necessary for salvation all those who, on the first Saturday of five consecutive months go to Confession and receive Holy Communion, recite five decades of the Rosary and keep Me company for a quarter of an hour while meditating on the mysteries of the Rosary, with the intention of making reparation to Me."

Jesus explained to Lucia that confession could be made within eight days or even longer, "provided they receive Me in the state of grace and have the intention of making reparation to the Immaculate Heart of Mary."

In June 1929, Our Lady appeared again to Lucia, in the Convent Chapel at Tuy, to ask (for) the Consecration of Russia to Her Immaculate Heart, promising by this means to prevent the spreading of its errors and to bring about its conversion.

In 1943 Our Lord appeared to Lucia and complained bitterly and sorrowfully that there are so small a number of souls who are willing to renounce whatever the observance of His law requires of them saying: "The sacrifice required of every person is the fulfillment of his duties in life and the observance of My law. This is the penance I now seek and require."

The Miracle of the Sun

The miracle of the sun has been described by Jesuit scientist Pio Sciatizzi as "the most obvious and colossal miracle in history." For the first time in 2,000 years, a major miracle had been predicted at a fixed time and place, enabling believers and freethinkers alike to witness it, "so that all the world may believe" as Our Lady stressed. As well as the 70,000 present in Fatima thousands of others over a 900 square mile area totally unconcerned about the events at Fatima also saw the sun dance in the sky and then plunge zig-zaggedly earthwards like a monstrous fireball. Both at Fatima and the surrounding area an estimated 100,000 people witnessed the miracle of the sun. "Facts are facts," wrote writer John D. Sheridan, "and the miracle of the sun is as authentic as the sinking of the Titanic," -- the Titanic witnessed by hundreds, the miracle at Fatima by tens of thousands.

The event is now part of documented history. Nowhere is it more graphically described than in the anti-clerical Portuguese press of the day. According to Francis Johnston in *"Have you Forgotten Fatima,"* Besides skeptical journalists, great numbers of unbelieving hostile intellectuals who had gathered at Fatima to ridicule a non-occurring miracle and witness the explosion of a myth, fell to their knees in floundering mud at the height of the overwhelming solar miracle and cried out unashamedly to the great God they had so vehemently denied.

"The sheer magnitude of the miracle -- something never experienced in recorded history -- and the deliberate pin-pointing of its exact time and location months in advance by the three children, drive one to the conclusion that God could only have performed it for the gravest of reasons. Of old, the warnings of God to a sinful world were conveyed by successive prophets. But at Fatima God warns us through the Queen of Prophets: 'The sins of the world are too great -- the punishment for sin is war -- men must cease to offend God and ask pardon for their sins' if the world was to find unity and peace... "The occurrences were characterized by Pope Paul VI as an affirmation of the Gospel. They constitute a unique confirmation of the Faith for today, reaffirming the Gospel doctrines of Heaven, Hell, sin, reparation, the Eucharist, the Communion of Saints, the existence of the Angels, and above all, the spiritual necessity of daily duty -- the acceptance of God's will in all things.

New stress was laid on devotion to the Mother of God, as a source of strength both for entering into the Gospel message and for living it. 'If there is not a single doctrine that has not been questioned today neither is there a Truth of Faith that Fatima has not reaffirmed . . . it is the announcement of the Gospel to the present age,' the Bishop of Leiria told 300,000 pilgrims at Fatima on October 13th, 1975."

Chapter 2

THE ROOTS OF COMMUNISM

"From Morn to Noon he fell
From Noon to dewy Eve"
Milton's *Paradise Lost*

While we are at all times aware that we are dealing with Principalities and Powers, for the purposes of this study we see the errors which Our Lady said Russia would spread throughout the world as having taken root in the Reformation in England.

Lucifer said: "I will not serve."

Adam said: "I will not serve."

Henry VIII said: "I will not serve."

From the sixth to the fifteenth century, 900 years, England enjoyed what is known as the golden age of Christianity. In that Golden Age, life revolved around the Church, that is the life of the common people revolved around the Monastery in particular.

The monasteries possessed land. This was divided up into medium-sized farms, perhaps more correctly described as small farms, and leased to farmers on the most favorable and secure terms. The farmer would contribute each harvest a tithe of what he produced, as rent on the land. If he produced little or nothing he paid little or nothing. If he had a good harvest he gave the tithe. His tenure was of the most secure kind for he did not deal with a personal landlord who could sell his land or pass it on to an erring heir. The farmer had his lease from the monastery and was not the victim of any individual or of his personal whim.

The monks and nuns had vows of poverty, chastity and obedience. The purpose and meaning of their lives were found in their dedication to the welfare and protection of the common people, because they saw it as God's will to ensure a truly Christian state. This was a meaning and purpose of their vows.

The monasteries looked after the poor, the sick, the widow, the orphan. There was thus no need of State welfare, no need of State hospitals, orphanages, poorhouses, or schools. To find their God in the needy was the purpose of their lives. This was allied to a life of prayer and sacrifice, without which it would not have been possible to lead such unselfish lives.

A modern day example can be given of the miracles that can be performed when such dedication is applied to the use of land. Over a hundred years ago the Cistercians were granted a piece of land on the top of a mountain. It was as bare of edible grass as the shell of an egg and could only feed snipe and wild birds. Today it contains lush green pasture and tillage lands and produces the finest herds and crops in the country. The monastery is called Mount Melleray, Co. Waterford.

As time went on the rights of the ordinary people were guaranteed and reinforced by Magna Carta, the Charter of Checks and Balances, represented by the King, the Commons and the Church. Magna Carta was drawn up by the Catholic Archbishop of Canterbury, and fully accepted by the King and Commons as the best guarantee of fair play for King and Commoner alike. The Church, concerned with no law but God's law, interpreted and handed down by the Pope, was truly the guardian of the common people. The people had proof of this in the martyrdom of St. Thomas Becket. Henry II had said: "Who will rid me of this troublesome priest?" What Henry II really wanted was to be rid of the curbs Thomas was putting on the King in defense of the people's rights. Henry, however, did not realize that the martyrdom of Thomas would serve to make the people aware of the importance of the Church in defense of their rights. They showed their awareness in their pilgrimages to the tomb of St. Thomas, pilgrimages which often swelled to 50,000 at a time.

In all those 900 years there was no such word as pauper in the English language. The word pauper had to be invented after the so-called reforms came which brought an end to the role of the Church as the guardian of the people's rights. When the King (Henry VIII) became head of the Church in England the most important element in the checks and balances of Magna Carta was eliminated and became fused with that of the King. Instead of there being three elements of checks and balances, there were now only two, and the most important, that which owed allegiance to God alone, was gone. As a result, except for the privileged few, England became one massive, pauperized orphanage with its Mother, the Church, driven underground, England which had been the Dowry of Mary for 900 years.

The Reformation brought with it the dissolution of the monasteries. The effect of the dissolution of the Religious Houses in London is thus described by Dr. Sharpe *(London and the Kingdom,* p. 404), as quoted by William Cobbett in *A History of the Protestant Reformation,* p. 93: "The sudden closing of these institutions caused the streets to be thronged with the sick and the poor, and the small Parish Churches to be so crowded . . . there was scarce room left for the parishioners themselves. The City Authorities saw at once that something would have to be done if they wished to keep their streets clear of beggars and of invalids and not invite the spread of sickness by allowing infected persons to wander at large." One such place thus closed, described by Cobbett: "Saint Cross or Holy Cross, situated in a meadow about half a mile from Winchester, is a hospital, or place of hospitality, founded and endowed by a Bishop of Winchester about seven hundred years ago. Succeeding Bishops added to its endowment, till at last it provided a residence and suitable maintenance for 48 decayed (feeble) gentlemen with priests, nurses, and other servants and attendants; and, besides this, it made provision for a dinner every day for a hundred of the most indigent men in the city. These met daily in a hall . . . Each had a loaf of bread, three quarts of small beer, and two 'messes' for his dinner, and they were allowed to carry home that which they did not consume on the spot.

"The Reformation despoiled the working classes of their patrimony, it tore from them that which nature had assigned them; it robbed them of that relief for the necessitous which was theirs by right imprescriptible, and which had been confirmed to them by the Law of God and the Law of the Land. It brought a compulsory, a grudging, an unnatural mode of relief, calculated to make the poor and rich hate each other, instead of binding them together as the Catholic mode did, by the bonds of Christian charity." Cobbett, p. 94.

Here it is well to note that up to the time of the Reformation not one penny in taxes ever had to be raised for the relief of the poor. Later the phrase Poor Law Valuation entered the English language after it had introduced the word pauper.

Cobbett describes the change that came about as follows: "Go into any county, and survey, even at this day, the ruins of its perhaps 20 abbeys and priories, and then ask yourself 'What have we in exchange for these?' Go to the site of some once opulent convent. Look at the cloister, now become in the hands of the rackrenter the receptacle for dung, fodder and faggot-wood; see the hall where for ages the widow, the orphan, the aged and the stranger found a table ready spread; see a bit of the walls now helping to make a cattle shed, the rest having been hauled away to build a workhouse; recognize in the side of a barn a part of the once magnificent chapel . . . which once resounded with the vespers of the monks.

"Then look at the monasteries as causing, in some of the most important of human affairs, that fixedness

23

which is so much the friend of rectitude in morals, and which so powerfully conduces to prosperity, private and public. The Monastery was a Proprietor that never died; its tenantry had to do with a deathless landlord; its lands and houses never exchanged owners; its tenants were liable to none of the many uncertainties that other tenants were; its oaks had never to tremble at the axe of the squandering heir; its manors had not to dread a change of lords; its villagers had all been born and bred under its eye and care; their character was of necessity a thing of great value, and as such, would naturally be a subject of great attention. A monastery was the centre of a circle in the country, naturally drawing to it all that were in need of relief, advice and protection, and containing a body of men and women having no cares of their own, and having wisdom to guide the inexperienced, and wealth to relieve the distressed." Cobbett, ibid.

This then was the state of England when Henry VIII acceded to the throne.

Henry succeeded to a great and prosperous kingdom, a full treasury and a happy and contented people. He was 18 years old when his father Henry VII died in 1509. Having been made King, Henry immediately made arrangements to marry Catherine, a Spanish princess, to whom he was betrothed since June 25th, 1503.

Catherine had come to England in 1501 to marry Henry's brother, Arthur, whom she married on November 14th, 1501. Arthur was a weak and sickly boy, aged only 14 at the date of the marriage. He died less than five months later on April 2nd, 1502. The marriage was never consummated because of his age and frailty.

Because of canon law it was, however, necessary to obtain a dispensation before Henry and Catherine could lawfully marry, Henry and Arthur having been brothers. The dispensation had been given as far back as December 1503, by Pope Julius.

By all accounts Henry dearly loved Catherine who was beautiful and virtuous. The marriage was blessed with three sons and two daughters, only one of whom, Mary, who later became Queen Mary, lived to adulthood.

After 17 years of happy marriage Henry cast his eye on a young lady at the Court, named Anne Boleyn. Such things happen often, but now there was a difference. Anne was ambitious. She wanted nothing less than to become Queen. Adam had said "The woman tempted me". Now it was Henry's turn. There were difficulties, but Henry affected to see a loophole. Suddenly he came to realize that all those years he had been living in sin with Catherine and he feared for his eternal soul, this despite the fact that his own Council and the Pope unanimously and unhesitatingly approved the marriage and that a dispensation had been granted in 1503. In spite of all this Henry decided to apply to the Pope to divorce him from his Queen. In this he failed again and again. In fact Henry was warned by the Pope under pain of excommunication to send Anne away. In Dr. Bayley's *Life of Bishop Fisher* it is asserted that Anne was actually Henry's daughter and that Lady Boleyn, her mother, said to the King when he was about to marry Anne "Sir, for the reverence of God, take heed what you do in marrying my daughter, for, if you record your conscience well, she is your own daughter as well as mine." To which the King replied: "Whose daughter soever she is, she shall be my wife." This may or may not have been true, though it is asserted in other publications and Sander's *Anglican Schism* states: "at least by the confession of the King and both Houses of Parliament Anne Boleyn was Henry's child."

Henry was really reluctant to break with the Pope and spent in all about six years in his fruitless quest. For the last three years Henry had Anne "under his protection" when she became, for the first time, with child. Now there was no time to be lost in order to make "an honest woman of her." A private marriage took place in January 1533. There was an urgency to make the marriage public, and for this Henry needed an accomplice.

In his own way Henry loved the Church, otherwise he would not have waited five to six years before breaking with the Pope. If in that time even a sizeable minority of the Bishops had steadfastly opposed Henry, as the Pope had, the King would have backed away from the final break and dealt with Anne in a much more humane way than he was to do a short time later when it didn't worry him to send her to the block.

Cranmer was the accomplice. In April 1533, he wrote a letter to the King, begging him, for the good of the nation, mind, and for the safety of his own soul, to grant him permission to try the question of the divorce, and beseeching him no longer to live in the peril attending an "incestuous intercourse", and on Friday, May 23rd, Cranmer as Primate declared the marriage of Henry and Catherine to have been null from the beginning. At Lambeth, Cranmer held another Court declaring that he was doing so by his pastoral and judicial authority, which he derived from the successors of the Apostles. Later by the same authority, he was to declare this marriage null and void from the beginning and to declare Anne's daughter, Elizabeth, a bastard.

With only one Bishop, Bishop Fisher, to oppose Henry, he was to have little trouble in persuading Parliament to recognize the King of England to be also Head of the Church there. He was now master of all the property of the Church, including that of the monasteries. What a temptation for Henry and his ignoble men. The grace of God to overcome tempta-tion was there for Henry and his abettors at all times, but God cannot, and will not, force anyone, King or commoner, to accept His Grace. Therein lies our freewill, our tragedy and our hope. We change the course of history for good or evil by our acceptance or rejection of the Grace of God. In our own day we see the course of history being changed by people who said yes to God and then being showered to overflowing with His Graces. One is Mother Theresa of Calcutta, Apostle of dying humanity thrown in the dustbin. The other is Frank Duff, Founder of the Legion of Mary, who in his own lifetime was to see in every diocese of the world a group of laypeople come together under the guidance of Mary to win the world for Christ, more dedicated and more selfsacrificing than any Roman soldier for his Emperor.

But we must get back to Henry. If a pebble can loose an avalanche, Henry by his rejection of the Grace of God loosed an avalanche of evil on the whole world, of which we may now be seeing the culmination, if we are lucky, and are spared worse.

Power corrupts, and absolute power corrupts absolutely, according to the historian. By making himself Head of the Church, and thus annihilating the most important check on power, that which owed allegiance only to God, and having the sword and gibbet at his command, Henry mounted on a roller coaster of destruction not only for himself but for his people.

The year is 1536. The King, "as Head of the Church" ordered his Archbishop, Cranmer, to hold his "spiritual Court" and to divorce him from Anne. Cranmer had previously declared the marriage with Anne "to be lawful, and had confirmed it by his authority, judicial and pastoral, which he derived from the successors of the Apostles." Now he was about to annul this marriage, on Henry's orders, and to declare it unlawful. Cranmer cited the King and Queen to appear in his "Court". The citation stated that their marriage had been unlawful, and that they were living in adultery and that, for the salvation of their souls they should come and show cause why they should not be separated.

Now, dear reader, please note the dates carefully. This was May 17th, but two days earlier, on May

15th, Anne had been condemned to death, and on May 19th Anne was executed.

Cranmer wound up the Court by saying: "in the name of Christ, and for the honor of God that the marriage was, and always had been, null and void." Note well this point, if her marriage had been null and void how could she have been guilty of adultery and treason (as the King's wife) for which she was so summarily beheaded? On the 15th she is condemned as the wife of the King, on the 17th she is pronounced never to have been his wife, and on the 19th she is executed for having been his unfaithful wife. Truly people in high places, if they fear not God, can do and say what they like.

On the very next day Henry married Jane Seymour at Marevell Hall in Hampshire. Thus began the "Reformation" to oppose which St. Thomas More and St. John Fisher shed their innocent blood.

How did evil triumph so easily? Edmund Burke says all that is necessary for the triumph of evil is that good men do nothing. A lot of good men must have sat and done nothing at this juncture or the course of history would have been different. It is the duty of those who can to defend helpless innocence against attacks of powerful guilt. Unfortunately helpless innocence was left to fend for itself. To deny the King's supremacy in favor of the Pope now became high treason, and to refuse to take an oath acknowledging the King's supremacy was deemed a denial of it. For this More and Fisher died.

Henry having used the precedent of using "Courts" and Acts of Parliament to legalize crime, virtually any crime in the book could become the law of the land, and so the day came in 1967 when the most innocent and defenseless of all human beings, the unborn child, was legally sentenced to death, and as in Henry's day, there was not even a whimper of dissent from the Catholic Bishops, but when there seemed to be a danger that euthanasia would be legalized there was a faint protest. Would the protest have been out of fear of purely personal safety? The time bomb ticks for all. No St. Thomas More, no Bishop Fisher to defend the innocent, defenseless unborn. Is abortion the ultimate in savagery? Can evil devise anything worse?

On mainland Europe the rot had set in, in 1517. The Pope had granted an indulgence, remission of temporal punishment due to sin, on condition of prayer, penance and the sacrifice of a contribution to the building of St. Peter's in Rome. To make this known was entrusted to the Order of Dominicans. One Martin Luther, an Augustinian Friar, with vows of poverty, chastity and obedience, took upon himself the mission of "reforming" the Church against what he regarded as an abuse. Like Henry, once he rejected the Grace of God, he too was to mount on a roller coaster of destruction. Though vowed to celibacy he took to himself a wife, and later was to give the Landgrave of Hesse a licence to have two wives at one and the same time.

Henry at this time being happily married opposed Luther to the point of writing a book, with the aid of St. Thomas More, against Luther. For this Henry was declared "Defender of the Faith" a title which pleased him very much. All this was of course before he was about to say: The Woman tempted me.

His new Queen, Jane Seymour, died on the birth of his son, Edward VI. Now, having a son for a successor he, with his Parliament (no Church to keep checks and balances), enacted that both Mary and Elizabeth, his two daughters, were illegitimate, and that in case of want of lawful issue the King should be enabled, by letters patent or by his last will, to give the crown to whomsoever he pleased.

In fine, it was enacted in 1537, in the 28th year of his reign, that except in cases of mere private right "the King's proclamation should be of the same force as an Act of Parliament". Where was Magna Carta now? The King was made in a great measure independent of Parliament by two statutes, one of which gave to his proclamations the force of law, the other appointed a tribunal consisting of 9 Privy Councillors, with power to punish all transgressors of such proclamations (Lingard Henry VIII as quoted by Cobbett on p. 77). Thus all law and justice were laid prostrate at the feet of a single man, an adulterer and a murderer.

One temptation led to another for Henry and his ignoble henchmen. More tempting than any woman was the wealth of the monasteries, which now became the focus of eyes glazed with avarice. The monasteries were wealthy. Living the most ordered lives, filled with prayer and work, living the most frugal lives themselves, anything left over from looking after the poor, the sick and the needy, went to enriching the monastery. Year after year additions were made in the shape of beautiful vestments, vessels of gold and silver, stained glass. There were beautiful manuscripts, richly adorned, all offered up in prayerful dedication to the Glory of God. Imagine a group of spoilt, greedy, ill-mannered children let loose on a candy store! In place of the candy, avarice now beheld gold and silver. The Fifth and Sixth Commandments had been eradicated from the Decalogue. Now it was the turn of the Seventh. Adultery had been legalized. Now nationwide robbery and plunder were to be legalized. The monasteries were the schools, free be it noted, the hospitals, the institutions responsible for the welfare of the widow, the orphan, the poor and the needy. Because the people depended on the Government for none of these things, the Government's power over the people was to that extent limited. Depend on a Government for all things, then that Government is all-powerful.

The monasteries had land. All historians agree they were easy landlords. They let their lands at low rents and on lease of long terms of years so that the farmers regarded themselves as a species of proprietors, always taking care to renew their leases before they expired. Thus was created a class of yeomen, real yeomen, independent of the aristocracy. This class was totally destroyed by the Reformation. As befitted their calling the monks did everything in the very best manner, their gardens, fishponds, farms all were attended by men seeking perfection in their work.

Just as Henry needed an ally in the matter of the divorce, now he needed one in his take-over bid for the monasteries. How often do we hear of the sinister take-over bid today when the small business is being gobbled-up? The take-over has caught on, and of course it is all quite legal as it was in Henry's day.

In the take-over of the monasteries Henry's ally was one Thomas Cromwell, now created Royal Vice-regent and Vicar-General of the new Head of the English Church. He was created a Peer. He was before the Primate in Parliament, he sat above all the bishops in assemblies of the clergy. He took precedence over all nobles, whether in office or out of office.

Cromwell began by setting on foot a visitation of the monasteries. The object was to obtain grounds of accusation against the monks and nuns. Suitable agents were not wanting to make the kind of visitation required. Into those havens of peace and tranquility they entered demanding an instant production of their title deeds, money and jewels. They menaced their innocent victims with charges of high treason, and they wrote in their reports not what they found, but that which they were required to write. The monks and nuns had no experience of such a visitation. They had no idea that Magna Carta and all the laws of the land could be set aside in a moment. Their sheltered and peaceful lives rendered them wholly unfitted to cope with such visitors, or with such crafty and desperate villainy.

The accused parties had no means of making a defense; there was no Court for them to appear in;

they dared not, even if they had the means, offer a defense or make a complaint, for they had seen the horrible consequences, the burnings, the rippings up of all those of their brethren who had dared dissent from any dogma or decree of the tyrant King.

The sole object was to despoil people of their property; and yet the parties from whom the property was to be taken were to have no court in which to plead their cause, no means of obtaining a hearing, could make no complaint but at the peril of their lives. They, the poor, the orphan, the widow, the handicapped, all of whom depended on them were to be at once stripped of this great mass of property without any other grounds than that of reports made by men sent for the express purpose of finding a pretense for the dissolution of the monasteries, and for the King taking to himself property that had never belonged to him, or to his predecessors.

On reports obtained by Cromwell and his Agents an Act of Parliament was passed in March, 1536, for the suppression, that is to say, the confiscation, of 376 monasteries, and for granting their estates, real and personal, to the King and his heirs. He took plate, jewels, gold and silver images and ornaments. However base as the Parliament was and full of greedy plunderers, it was not passed without some opposition. According to Spelman's History of Sacrilege "the Bill stuck long in the Lower House and could get no passage, when the King commanded the Commons to attend him in the forenoon in his gallery, where he let them wait till late in the afternoon, and then, coming out of his chamber, walking a turn or two amongst them and looking angrily at them, first on one side and then on the other, said at last: 'I hear that my Bill will not pass, but I will have it pass, or I will have some of your heads' and without other rhetoric returned to his chamber. Enough was said -- the Bill passed, and all was given to him as he desired." Shades of Stalin as reported again and again by those who stood in his presence when he was at the top. Power corrupts and absolute power . . .

Thus, the King, his heirs and assigns, acquired the whole of this vast property, to do and use to their own wills, *and to the pleasure of Almighty God*, and to the honor and profit of the realm. The things that are done in God's Name! !

Besides the lands and houses and stock this tyrannical Act gave Henry the household goods, the gold and silver and jewels, and every other thing belonging to the monasteries. Thus was Magna Carta broken, the monks and nuns were robbed, and lastly the indigent, the widow, the orphan and the stranger were left defenseless, and robbed with the monks and nuns. The parties robbed, even the actual possessors of the property, were never heard in their defense. There was no charge against any particular convent. The charges were loose and general, and levelled against all convents whose revenues did not exceed a certain sum. There was a reason for a 'certain sum'.

The reason for stopping at that point was that there was yet something to be done with the nobles and gentry before a general seizure of the great monasteries could be safely attempted. The weak were first attacked, but the means were very soon found for attacking and sacking the remainder. With Magna Carta gone might now became right, as it is to this very day, only today the con-men on words make it sound less crude.

The moment Henry got possession of these Church lands and estates he began to grant them away to his "assigns" as the Act calls them.

Before four years had passed Henry found himself as poor as if he had never confiscated a single convent, so sharp were the pious reformers and so eager "to please Almighty God". When he complained to Cromwell, the latter reminded him that there was much more to come. "Tut, tut, man, my whole realm would not staunch their maws" was the King's reply. Nevertheless he went ahead with the seizure of the larger monasteries. An Act was passed (31 Henry VIII, Chap. 13) giving all these surrendered monasteries to the King, his heirs and assigns, and also all other monasteries, and all hospitals and colleges into the bargain. As Cobbett remarked the carcasses being thus laid prostrate, the rapacious vultures who had assisted in the work flew on it and began to tear it to pieces. The people here and there rose in insurrection, but deprived of leadership there was no hope for them. Their natural leaders had sided with the tyrant. I quote Cobbett's *History of the Protestant Reformation,* p. 174:

"Tyrants have often committed robberies on their people, but in all cases but this, in England at least, there was always something of legal process observed. In this case there was no such thing. The base Parliamentarians who were to share, and who did most largely share in the plunder, had given not only the lands and houses to the tyrant, or rather, had taken them to themselves, but had disposed, in the same short way, of all the moveable goods, stock on farms, crops, and which was of more consequence, of the gold, silver and jewels. Let the reader judge of the ransackings that now took place . . . the people in those days were honest enough to suffer all these things, to remain in their places without a standing army and without even police officers.

"Never in all probability since the world began was there so rich a harvest of plunder. The ruffians of Cromwell (Thomas) entered the convents, they tore down the altars to take away the gold and silver, ransacked the chests and drawers of the monks and nuns, tore off the covers of books that were ornamented with precious metals. These books were all in manuscript. Single books had taken in many cases half a long lifetime to compose and to copy out fair (in good style). Whole libraries, the getting of which together had taken ages upon ages and had cost immense sums of money, were scattered abroad by these hellish ruffians, when they had robbed the covers of their rich ornaments. The ready money in the convents, down to the last shilling, was seized. . . and this, observe, towards persons, women as well as men, who had committed no crime known to the law, who had no crime regularly laid to their charge, who had no hearing in their defense, the whole of whose possessions was guaranteed to them by Magna Carta as much as the King's crown was to him, and whose estates were enjoyed for the benefit of the poor . . ."

Canterbury was the cradle of English Christianity and to Canterbury now the reformers hastened. It was rich in altars, tombs, gold and silver images, together with diamonds and other precious stones. Also at Canterbury were the tombs of St. Austin and St. Thomas à Becket. This shrine offered a plenteous booty to the plunderers. Becket, who was Archbishop of Canterbury in the reign of Henry II lost his head for resisting the King when he was preparing to rob the Church, and enslave and pillage the people. The people looked to him as a martyr to their liberties as well as their religion. His crime was that he defended Magna Carta against the King. Pilgrimages to his tomb were never ending, often swelling to 100,000 people. Offerings poured in. Hospitals and other pious establishments were dedicated to him, most notably St. Thomas Hospital. Such offerings made this shrine exceedingly rich and magnificent. A King of France had given it a diamond said to be the most valuable in Europe.

The gold, the silver, the jewels, filled two chests, each of which required six to eight men of that day (when laborers used to have plenty of meat) to move them to the door of the Cathedral. Nothing in rapacity, in profligacy, in insolence, could have equalled this robbery. Henry's will was now law. He had eliminated the voice of the Church (the most important voice in the system of checks and balances to make fair laws) and he had bribed the peoples' remaining natural leaders to his side. All that remained of the monasteries and convents were the buildings. These were now pulled down with gunpowder. The whole country was thus disfigured giving the appearance of a land recently invaded by barbarians. Civilizations usually die from within, not from outside attack.

The name of Alfred is dear to all Englishmen. He taught his people by precept to be sober, industrious, brave and just. He promoted learning, founded the University of Oxford and introduced trial by jury. But even his tomb was desecrated and the Abbey and estates given to the Earl of Southampton.

The Catholic Church included in it a great deal more than the business of teaching religion and of practising worship and administering the Sacraments. It had a great deal to do with the temporal welfare of the people. It provided, and amply provided, for all the wants of the poor and the distressed . . . It contained a great body of land, proprietors whose revenues were distributed in various ways amongst the people at large, upon terms always singularly advantageous to the tenant. It was a great and powerful estate, independent both of the aristocracy and the Crown, and naturally siding with the people. But above all things, it was a provider for the poor and a keeper of hospitality . . . and held society together by ties of religion rather than by the tramels and terrors of the law. It was the great cause of that description of tenants called lifeholders, who formed a most important link in the chain of society, coming after the proprietors in fee and before the tenant at will, participating in some degree, in the proprietorship of the estate, and yet not wholly without dependence on the proprietor. This race of persons, formerly so numerous in England, became almost wholly extinct, their place having been supplied (taken) by a comparatively few rack-renters and by swarms of miserable paupers. The Catholic Church held the lending of money for gain to be directly in face of (against) the Gospel. It considered all such gain as usurious and, of course, criminal. Usury among Christians was wholly unknown until Henry VIII laid his hands on the property of the Church and the poor.

Every Church altar had more or less gold and silver, censers, candlesticks, and other things used in the celebration of Mass. The Mass, therefore, had to go. There was no longer to be an altar, but a table. There was to be much quarrelling about where the table would stand, its shape, and whether it was to be placed to the north, the east, the west or the south, and whether the people were to stand, kneel or sit at it. Where have we been hearing all this again of late? England in a short space of time had become a den of thieves, where the miserable laborers were left to live on potatoes and water. When the Church lands became private property the rents were raised, the money spent at a distance from the estates, and the tenants exposed to the rapacity of stewards. How familiar it all sounds to Irish people! Whole estates were laid waste. The tenants were expelled. Even the cottagers were deprived of the commons on which they formerly fed their cattle. There was a great decay of the people, as well as a diminution of that former plenty.

Henry VIII was succeeded by his son Edward, a minor, who reigned for only a short time. He, in turn, was succeeded by Queen Mary. Queen Mary made every effort to restore Church property. But the plunder had been so immense, the plunderers were so numerous, they were so powerful, and there were so few families of any account who had not participated in deeds one way or another hostile to the Church that the Queen was up against almost impossible odds. The Mass was in all parts of the country once more celebrated, the people were no longer burnt with red hot irons and made slaves for merely asking alms, and they began to hope that England would be England again, and that hospitality and charity would return.

But there were the plunderers to deal with, and the Parliament. This was the Parliament that had declared Cranmer's (declaration of Henry VIII's) divorce of Catherine to be lawful thereby declaring Mary a bastard. Now this same Parliament was to declare Elizabeth a bastard, and Mary the lawful and legitimate Queen of England, and a little while later when Mary was dead and Elizabeth Queen it was to do another about turn. How true what one of the American Founding Fathers said: "Let me hear no more of confidence in man, but bind him down from mischief by the chains of the Constitution." I will conclude this chapter by a quotation from Pope Leo XIII's encyclical, *Quod Apostolici* published in 1878:

"Those venomous teachings (viz. the principles of the Protestant Reformation) like pernicious seed scattered far and wide among the nations have produced in course of time death-bearing fruit . . . Deriving

pretentiously its name from reason, this false doctrine
. . . has pervaded the whole of civilized society. Hence
. . . Governments have been organized without God
or His divinely established order being taken into
account. It has even been contended that public
authority . . . originates not from God, but from the
mass of the people, which, considering itself unfet-
tered by all divine sanction, refuses to submit to any
laws that it has not passed of its own free will . . . The
very Author and Redeemer of mankind has been
forced slowly and gradually to withdraw from the
scheme of studies at Universities, colleges and high
schools, as well as from all the practical working of
public life . . . the keen longing after happiness has
been narrowed down to the range of the present life .
. . No wonder that tranquility no longer prevails in
public life or private life, or that the human race has
been hurried onward well nigh to the verge of ruin."

Chapter 3

MONEY -- THE ROOT OF ALL EVIL

"I set to work to read the Act of Parliament by which the Bank of England was created in 1694. The inventors knew well what they were about. Their design was to mortgage by degrees the whole of the country, all the lands, all the houses, and all other property, and even all labor, to those who would lend their money to the State -- the scheme, the crafty, the cunning, the deep scheme has produced what the world never saw before -- starvation in the midst of plenty."

Wm. Cobbett in
A History of the Protestant Reformation

Our Lady said at Fatima that Russia would spread her errors throughout the world, would foment wars and that many nations would be lost. In the last Chapter we saw how the seeds of those errors were planted firmly in the so-called Reformation. Magna Carta was gone and with it the power of the Church to look after the poor and the needy. From a country without a standing army, hardly needing a police force, a standing army now became the order of the day. Kings came and went. Dictators came and went.

England had its Civil Wars. England had been called Merry England. Now the 900-year Golden Age of Christianity was gone forever.

The year 1690 saw the end of one of the Civil Wars in which the lawful King, James, was ousted and William, a foreign Prince, installed as King in the place of James. The decisive battle was fought in Ireland, ever since known as the Battle of the Boyne. To bring in a foreign prince to get rid of a country's lawful King is treason in any man's language, but as the poet put it, "if treason prosper, none dare call it treason." The real reason for bringing over William came to light four years later, in 1694. In that year the greatest confidence trick in the history of mankind was pulled off by a group of privateers led by one William Patterson. It was a deed that was to change the course of the history not only of England, but of the whole world. Once this good earth was sunk in water. Today it is sunk in debt and it all dates back to the year 1694. In that year Patterson and his friends went to the King, William, and put to him this proposition:

"We will lend you £1,200,000 in gold, at 8 per cent, provided you will give us a Charter whereby we are enabled to issue in notes £1,200,000 and lend it to the public at 8 per cent." This meant creating, or making, money out of nothing, being allowed to call it money, and to lend it to the public at a high interest rate. It was always the King's or the Emperor's head or stamp on whatever was used for money, that made it legal tender. Christ said: "Show me a coin of the realm, whose image has it? Give to Caesar the things that are Caesar's and to God the things that are God's."

Now this private syndicate decided that they would be Caesar only that nobody but they would know. Where heretofore the King or Emperor anywhere issued money responsibly as a token to represent whatever goods needed to be exchanged, and had his image stamped thereon to prove it, while sending it into circulation free of interest, this private syndicate persuaded, conned, blackmailed, call it what you like, the King to allow them to create (make out of nothing) £1,200,000 and lend it to the public at 8 per cent.

This was new money that had no backing of goods to be exchanged. It was the beginning of inflation, and eventually it led to a private syndicate acquiring a cast-iron monopoly over the supply and circulation of the money not just of England, but of the whole world, and as Cobbett remarked, produced what the world never saw before -- starvation in the midst of plenty. Today it is more true than ever that people are hungry in the midst of plenty, and it all dates back to this event in history. It was a turning point in history, and except for the privileged few who hold the control and the power, every man, woman and child the world over is contributing to the interest on the government debt then created.

Some time later this syndicate arrived at the idea of calling itself the Bank of England. It went on lending to the King, and every time it lent to the King a certain amount, by the charter it had obtained from the King, it printed paper money to the same amount which it lent to the public at interest, and all it cost those cunning folk was the cost of the paper, ink and the bookkeeping. Before long they had succeeded in persuading the King to take £16 million in gold from them and this entitled them to print £16 million in paper money and lend it to the public at interest.

If new money was needed to carry on the affairs of the State, the Government could have done the sensible thing and, instead of borrowing, decided to issue its own paper money. It could likewise have done so at the mere cost of paper and printing. There would have been no need for interest to be paid to anybody, and the taxpayer would not have been burdened to provide interest.

Some time later the group that now called itself the Bank of England came up with a much smarter idea. It created paper money to the tune of ten times the amount of gold it held and lent it to the public at interest. Soon this private monopoly, calling itself the Bank of England, acquired total power over the country's money supply, occupying a far more powerful position than the King and Commons.

During the first half of the 19th century the commercial banks invented and began to use "check" money because they were stopped (from) printing their own notes. This new kind of money did not exist even in the form of paper notes, but was brought into being by the simple process, either of entering in bank books the figures recording the granting of loans, or of filling in checks to enable the banks to buy themselves securities. These checks, it is important to note, did not, like a private individual's check, draw on and transfer money already in existence, they created new money to the value of the figures written on them.

In the 1914-18 war it was easy for the banks to *create* vast sums of money and either "lend" it to the government or allow their wealthy customers to buy War Loan with it and share the interest in the ratio of banks 4 per cent to nominees 1 per cent. Naturally the value of the pound dropped, and in four years it had fallen to exactly half. In 1914 the national debt was £700 millions. By 1920 it was £7,000 millions and the banks held approximately 90 per cent of the War Loan. The vast sums paid to the banks in interest precipitated the industrial crisis of the 1920's and 1930's and led to the 1939-45 War which was secretly planned. This will be dealt with in a later chapter.

In 1934-5 total receipts from income tax were £229,214,963. Interest on the national debt paid in that year was £211,657,232. In 1935-6 income tax receipts were £237,362,332 and the interest on the national debt was £211,533,776. In those two years out of income taxes of £446 millions only £43 millions were available to the government for the many services required by the people. Moreover, nearly 70 per cent of the national debt was created (made out of nothing) by, and held by, the banks.

If the national debt is not to hang forever like a millstone round the necks of the people is there anything that can be done about it, and all its attendant evils? The answer is simple but not easy.

In the first place, a clear distinction should be drawn between those who have bought their holdings of the national debt with money saved, earned, inherited, or otherwise normally acquired; and those who have bought their holdings with newly-created money, i.e. the banks and those bankers' nominees who have been granted bank loans wherewith to make their purchases. Banks should be ordered to sell their holdings of government securities to the state, which, as a matter of bookkeeping, would pay them with newly-created non-debt money. This money, in accordance with existing banking practice, the banks would then be required to destroy, for, just as under the present system they create new money when making loans or buying securities, so do they destroy money when they get repayment of the principal of loans, or sell securities, keeping only the interest for themselves.

If this action were taken, a part of the national debt would be wiped out immediately, without any risk of inflation. No injustice would have been inflicted even on the banks for they have already done extremely well out of the interest received in the past from government securities which were purchased neither with their depositors' money nor with money they had to save or earn.

With regard to bankers' nominees, i.e. those to whom the banks have lent newly-created money to enable them to buy government securities, these, where they exist, should be dealt with in a rather similar way. The banks should be directed to call in their loans made to these nominees. The government would then give the nominees newly-created, non-debt money to enable them to make repayment, and the banks, on receipt of the money, would, again in accordance with present practice, cancel and destroy it.

There would remain only that part of the national debt purchased by private individuals, organizations, etc.; with money already in existence and obtained in a normal manner. These persons should be paid the full value of their holdings with newly-created non-debt money, as rapidly as could be arranged without risk of inflation, and they could then spend the money so received or invest it in industry. It might be found possible and desirable to speed up the process by granting fewer bank loans during the period when it was carried out. The less money created by bank loans the more can safely be created for other purposes.

If the question be asked: "How can the government obtain the money which it formerly got by borrowing at interest?", the answer is very simple. It can direct the banks to create it not in the form of interest-bearing debt, and it can use anti-inflation taxation to collect, from time to time, just as much of that money as may be necessary to prevent an excess from remaining in circulation beyond the total of goods and services to be bought with it.

The U.S. Federal Reserve Bank is a money dictatorship possessing absolute autocratic powers over the American people and indirectly over the rest of the world. The parallel between the set-up of the Federal Reserve System and that of the Communist Party in Russia is startling.

In the USSR a tightly knit clique of the Communist Party runs everything, operating in total secrecy and with total disregard for the people and for the Constitution of the U.S. In both countries, a small group of people have knowledge of, and benefit from, the decisions of those tightly knit cliques.

In the U.S. monetary policy is controlled by the seven members of the Federal Reserve Board, the 12 Presidents, and the 108 directors of the 12 Federal Reserve Banks. These 127 people, operating in total secrecy, have absolute power over monetary decisions.

In the USSR there are 133 members of the Central Committee of the Communist Party. This group runs everything in the USSR.

Both these bodies have a more élite group -- a small super committee.

In the Federal Reserve System the group is known as the Open Market Committee, composed of 7 members of the Federal Board and 5 of the 12 Presidents of the Federal Reserve Banks -- 12 in all -- with the other seven presidents participating.

In the USSR there is a small committee within the Central Committee known as the Politburo. This has 11 members as compared with the Open Market Committee of 12.

When the Open Market Committee meets every three weeks in Washington it goes behind locked doors. The shades are drawn and special guards are put in the hall to guard against any possible intrusion. Nothing is known of what goes on at the meetings until 6 years later after the statute of limitations has run on any crime that might have been committed. It is in these sessions that the monetary decisions, interest rates, and the money supply are decided. Not even the President of the U.S. can attend these secret meetings. Such is democracy U.S. style.

In the USSR the Politburo meets several times a month in Moscow in totally secret sessions. No one is allowed past the armed guards. As in the U.S. the decisions of the Politburo are kept secret until the Party decides to release the information.

The Communist Party takes care of its friends in Russia, and in the U.S. the Federal Reserve takes care of its banker friends. In both places the people are shut out. Only an élite few get the benefit.

That 240 million supposedly free Americans should stand for such an absurd situation seems incredible. It is not so incredible when one understands the depth of their ignorance of what is going on at the top. Those millions of people are treated as if they were retarded children whose guardians at the top know what is best for them. In 20 years in business, for about five months of the year, it was my privilege to meet Americans almost every day. Never losing an opportunity of testing their knowledge of the Conspiracy and the power of the money controllers, in all those years I only met one person who knew anything at all of the power that controlled their lives. He was a Government employee in the State of Massachusetts. The one fear the Insiders have is of being exposed and anyone who dares such a venture can expect to be smeared, even to death.

The World Bank, the Export-Import Bank, the International Monetary Fund, are all instruments created by the Insiders for the control of the human race.

The International Monetary Fund was set up at Bretton Woods in 1944. Its architect was Harry Dexter White, a known Communist spy. President Truman was informed by the FBI of his Communist associations but instead of having him arrested he promoted him to the International Monetary Fund, along with a number of other high-ranking Communist spies. They were Frank Coe, Laughlin Currie, William Ullman, Nathan Silvermaster and Alger Hiss. All had had top jobs in the American State Department and enjoyed direct Presidential immunity from exposure. Why should a President of the US want to protect a Communist spy? There is only one answer: the President like the spy takes his orders. Each knows which way the world is shaping. The theme of Professor Quigley's *Tragedy and Hope* is that we are now too far along the road to World Dictatorship to turn back. In the *Saturday Evening Post* of October 18, 1944, following the meeting at Bretton Woods, a spokesman for the Insiders, Peter Drucker, wrote:

"Should the world adopt a controlled economic system, leadership would logically fall to the Soviet Union. Russia would be the model for such a dictatorship, for Russia was the first country to develop the technique of international economic control."

The International Monetary Fund claims sovereignties, immunities and privileges superseding those of the member nations which comprise the Fund and within the territories of its member nations.

Section 2, Article IX, provides that the Fund shall possess full juridical personality, and, in particular, the capacity: (1) to contract; (2) to acquire and dispose of immovable and movable property; (3) to institute legal proceedings.

In this one Article the Fund gains the power to judge, determine their status and enforce their own decisions, reducing the member state to the status of policeman. Section 10 of Article IX directs each nation to enforce the principles of the Article in terms of its own law, and report the action taken to the Fund.

Section 3, Article IX prohibits the Fund from being sued in the Courts of any state or country where it is located, except where it expressly waives that immunity.

Section 4, Article IX states: "The property and assets of the Fund, wherever located and by whomsoever held, shall be immune from search, confiscation, expropriation, or any other form of seizure by executive or legislative action."

Section 7, Article IX gives the Fund the same diplomatic immunity as any other nation with consular representation, with the exception that representatives of other nations can be asked to leave.

Section 8, Article IX gives immunities and privileges to Officers and Employees. Part (2) of the Section states: "All Governors, Executive Directors, Alternates, Officers and employees NOT BEING LOCAL NATIONALS shall be granted the same immunities from immigration restrictions, alien registration requirements and national service obligations, and the same facilities as regards exchange restrictions as are accorded by members to the representatives, officials and employees of comparable rank of other members."

Sections 1 and 9 of Article IX exempt from taxation all assets, property income, operations and transactions, as well as the salaries and emoluments paid by the Fund to the Executive Directors, Alternates, Officers and employees of the Fund WHO ARE NOT LOCAL CITIZENS, LOCAL SUBJECTS, OR OTHER LOCAL NATIONALS.

Also exempt from taxation is any obligation or security issued by the Fund, including any interest or dividend.

History has recorded that when great civilizations fell into ruins never to rise again the wealth of those civilizations was in the hands of a few.

John Adams wrote as follows to Thomas Jefferson: "All the perplexities, confusions, and distresses in America arise, not from defects in the Constitution or confederation, not from want of honor or virtue, as much as from downright IGNORANCE of the nature of coin, credit, and circulation."

In reply Jefferson said: ". . . And I sincerely believe, with you, that Banking establishments are more dangerous than standing armies; and that the principle of spending money to be paid by posterity, under the name of funding is but swindling futurity on a large scale." Meyer Amschel Rothschild said: "Permit me to issue and control the money of a nation, and I care not who makes its laws."

The gold in Fort Knox does not belong to the American people, but to the Federal Reserve, a privately owned body. The names of those who own stock in it have never been revealed.

Money, it must never be forgotten, derives its value from the presence in the country of an adequate backing of goods and services. It does not derive any value from the fact that it was first created as interest-bearing debt, or indeed, debt of any kind.

According to Gibbon, the decline and fall of the Roman Empire was caused by the evils of inflation, a permissive society and a rush from the land to the cities. They are all with us now, and 1984 is round the corner. (I am indebted to Abundance, the Social Credit Centre, Montagu Chambers, Mexborough, South Yorks, for the subject matter of dealing with government loans.)

As regards the flight from the land many believe this is a natural phenomenon. Not so. In 1900 eleven per cent of the people of the United States lived in cities, and eighty-nine per cent lived on the land. By

1970, in just two short generations, the ratio was exactly reversed. Eleven per cent of the people lived on the land and eighty- nine per cent in the cities.

By now, the 1980's, well over 90 per cent of the people of the U.S. live in cities. It was deliberate policy to get people off the land, the one spot on earth on which they have most independence.

In any city, if a government or a dictatorship has control of both water and electricity it takes very little time to bring people to their knees if both are cut off for any reason. In *The Wanderer*, a weekly Catholic newspaper some years ago there was a full description of the plan formulated by the Communists for taking control of the U.S. by having their key men cut off water and light at a given moment in every city and town in the U.S.

In his book *Technological Terrorism,* recently published in the U.S. by Devin-Adair, Prof. R.C. Clark warns that "computers can be tapped like any telephone line" warning that "if the general rule is that the vulnerability of a nation or a metropolitan area is roughly proportional to its centralization, then the potential for havoc in this area (computers) is enormous."

The danger of technological centralization is accentuated by a financial policy of continuous inflation. Radical trade unionists are then in a position to hold nations to ransom. The individual finds it progressively more difficult to protect himself.

In a sane society technology would be used to serve the individual. But the first requirement is a financial policy which eliminates inflation. In a sane and Christian society that would be easy. What is physically possible can always be made financially possible. In this we are confronted by principalities and powers, and the key to the power that is enslaving mankind is the total power held by a tiny clique over the creation and circulation of money, and it all began in 1694 when King William, the Dutchman, usurper of the British throne allowed himself to be either conned or blackmailed into giving a charter to a group of privateers to make money by a stroke of the pen.

If only those who celebrate the Battle of the Boyne really understood what they are celebrating. In 1694 King William became head of the London branch of the Masonic Order, a highly secret society reputed to be the parent of Communism. Would this have been King William's reward for the charter which gave rise to the financial enslavement of the whole world, where millions starve in the midst of plenty?

The following letter was addressed in 1943 to His Excellency, Most Rev. William Godfrey, the Apostolic Delegate to Great Britain, to the Anglican Archbishops of Canterbury, York and Wales, and to other ecclesiastical dignitaries in Britain. It was accompanied by a proposal to form an association having for object an honest national money system for England. The letter runs as follows:

"Your Grace,

1. We, all of British blood and descent, having studied the fundamental causes of the present world unrest, have long been forced to the conclusion that

an essential first step towards the return of human happiness and brotherhood with economic security and liberty of life and conscience, such as will permit the Christian ethic to flourish again, is the immediate resumption by the community in each nation of its prerogative over the issue of money including its modern credit substitutes.

2. This prerogative has been usurped by those still in general termed "bankers" both national and international, who have perfected a technique to enable themselves to create the money they lend by the granting of bookkeeping credits, and to destroy it by the withdrawal of the latter at their discretion, in accordance with entirely mistaken and obsolete ideas which they do not defend against impartial and informed scientific criticism and examination. In this way a form of national money debt has been invented, in which the lender surrenders nothing at all; and which it is physically an impossibility for the community ever to pay. Any attempt to do so produces the artificial "economic blizzard", as it did after the 1914-18 war.

3. This has led to the gradual rise of a form of national, international and supra-national power, dominating through its monopolization of the national social credit all the basic creative activities of mankind. Thus, in this as in other countries, it has become impossible to obtain publication in the press, or to broadcast on the radio, the truth concerning this economic enslavement which holds the peoples of the world in thrall.

4. Under the world's present financial system, money, except for a now trifling proportion, is originally created by the issue of a loan at interest by the "bankers" who lend nothing themselves but in effect make a forced levy in kind on the nation by conferring on the borrower the power to purchase a corresponding amount of wealth on the market, which wealth does not belong to them, or those who borrow from them, but to the community. The proceeds of the issue of new money -- whether of paper or any other form of credit money -- belong to the nation in which it is, or is accepted as, legal tender, and not to the issuer. Herein lies the basic flaw of the existing monetary system.

5. By this method, which has come to be regarded as legal by virtue of established practice, the banks in our country are responsible for the issue of new money of their own creation amounting today to between two and three thousand million pounds -- this being the difference between loans extended, including those to themselves, and those repaid since they instituted the system a number of years ago -- and are therefore extracting by means of interest an annual tribute from the nation of over £100,000,000 for what has now become to them a relatively costless and riskless service. But the real danger, well understood in every preceding era of history, is the undermining of all lawfully constituted authority by the creation and destruction of money carried on in secret for private gain and the acquisition of power.

6. All forms of government, whether conservative, liberal or labour, fascist, socialist, or Communist, fall alike under the control of a political power group, which is ultimately, and in large measure unwittingly, dominated by the money creators and manipulators. In this way the national political power, which, if the individual is to enjoy the maximum of personal freedom consistent with his duty to his conscience and his fellows, should be distributed throughout the people, has been usurped without their knowledge or consent.

7. It will be seen that the present monetary system, which by its disregard of primary physical and ethical laws is inevitably destroying the civilization into which it has been introduced, requires rectification both in its material technique and in the ethics which at present inspire and control this technique. It is particularly in view of its devastating effects in the moral sphere that we have ventured to refer to ecclesiastical authority, and to invoke the churches to action.

8. We therefore appeal to you in your position of great authority and influence to proclaim the truth to the nation on this subject and in the hope that you may see fit to disseminate as widely as possible the text of this statement, whereby this vitally important question may be brought to the light of day and earnestly enquired into by the peoples of the British Commonwealth.

9. We do so in all Christian fellow-feeling, knowing and honoring the efforts you make against the

abuses of our present economic system and the evils of usury, and believing that the world is now in the gravest crisis of its history. The issue of new money by the moneylender is an unforeseen result of the modern check as a substitute for national money -- a valuable invention which in itself was undoubtedly social and benevolent in intention and effect. If the check system were corrected, as it can be simply corrected, to restore to the nations their rightful prerogative over the issue of money, there is every reason to retain it.

We fully appreciate the services which banking organizations have rendered and can continue to render to the community. But the issue and destruction of money by the moneylender is not a service but a weapon which can be and has been used to perpetuate poverty amidst abundance, which renders individuals and nations powerless to protect themselves, and which may even be perverted to serve vast designs for the complete subjugation of the human race to tyranny, exploitation and the powers of darkness and evil."

The letter was signed by thirty-two of the most eminent men in public life in England, one of them Frederick Soddy, MA, LID, FRS, Nobel Laureate in Chemistry, author of *Wealth, Virtual Wealth and Debt, Money versus Man and the Role of Money*.

In a covering letter, signed by Norman A. Thompson and Professor Soddy, it was stated that "if the way is not already paved before the cessation of hostilities towards a saner economic system under which all members of the nation will receive a more equitable and humane treatment, the return of our countrymen serving in the forces, who are becoming increasingly aware of the injustices of the existing monetary system is likely to be the prelude to uncompromising disturbances."

A shortened version of the above letter appeared recently in *The Word* magazine as follows: "We, having studied the fundamental causes of the present world unrest, have long been forced to the conclusion that an essential first step towards the return of human happiness and brotherhood with economic security and liberty of life and conscience, such as will permit the Christian ethic to flourish again, is the immediate resumption by the community in each nation of its prerogative over the issue of money, including its modern credit substitutes. This prerogative has been usurped by those still termed "bankers", both national and international, who have perfected a technique to enable themselves to create the money they lend by the granting of bookkeeping credits, and to destroy it by the withdrawal of the latter at their discretion. In this way a form of national money debt has been invented, in which the lender surrenders nothing at all; and which it is physically an impossibility for the community ever to pay."

This country, the 26-county Republic of Ireland, started off without any debt. Now it is more than eight billion in debt, and everyone from the child in the cradle to the old age pensioner is taxed one way or another to pay just the interest. Recently it was stated that more than eighty per cent of all PAYE taxes goes to pay the interest on our national debt alone. We will have gone a long way towards solving our economic problems when we can name the receivers of such vast sums, and the means by which ownership was acquired.

Sir Josiah Stamp, Director of the Bank of England, made the following statement two generations ago:

"Banking was conceived in iniquity and born in sin . . . Bankers own the earth. Take it away from them, but leave them the power to create money, and, with the flick of a pen, they will create enough money to buy it all back again . . . Take this power away from them and all great fortunes like mine will disappear and they ought to disappear for then this would be a better and a happier world to live in . . . But if you want to continue to be the slaves of Bankers and pay the cost of your own slavery, then let Bankers continue to create money and control credit."

Sir Josiah, later Lord Stamp, was equally frank about the subject of taxation. He said: "While a few years ago no one would have believed it possible that a scale of taxation such as that at present existing could be imposed upon the British public without revolution, I have every hope that with skillful education and propaganda this scale can be very considerably raised."

Lest it be supposed that nationalization is the answer it is well to ponder the statement of another director of the Bank of England, Sir Montagu Norman, "Nationalization; why we welcome it." What he meant was that nothing was changed by changing the name over the door. What is evil is the monopoly. State monopoly simply means that the power of the monopolists is increased. A private monopoly of any kind is bad, but so long as it is divorced from the state, then Government may be used as a counterbalance. Which provokes the question of who owns the real credit of a community. The basic features of real credit are not, as the Marxists and their fellow-travellers teach, labor, but inheritance: basic capital, the cultural heritage, the division of labor and the tools and capital equipment bequeathed to one generation from previous generations. This real credit belongs to the individual members of any society -- the individual must have access to his own credit as a right -- under proper conditions.

To rob the individual of access to his own credit is like the State, or some other power, refusing the individual access to money or property which has been willed to him by his forebears. The correct function of the State is to uphold the Rule of Law -- to ensure that there is justice -- so that the individual can be free to gain access to his own credit. To insist that the individual must engage in some form of production -- even if only filling forms in a Government bureaucracy, a form of digging holes and filling them in again, before he can gain access to his own credit, is to impose conditions on how the individual is to use his real credit. It stems from the philosophy of totalitarianism. It reflects the textbook teachings of Marx and Keynes. The Banks have been nationalized in Poland but the people are hungry, and hunger for material food may possibly be the least of their miseries.

The present financial system feeds inflation and inflation is a direct assault on God's commandment -- Thou shalt not steal -- It is a more sophisticated form of stealing than straightforward physical robbery at the point of a gun, but it is stealing. What has happened recently in Ireland because of the Rent Restrictions Act is an admission that inflation is stealing. Inflation is a form of slavery, the taxation which feeds it is a form of slavery, engineered by a form of present day black magic from which the most intelligent people recoil terrified of asking the simplest questions concerning the probity of either. Truly the human race is like Gulliver tied down and helpless at the hands of a handful of little men with satanic power behind them. The gentle Christ made a whip to drive the moneychangers out of the Temple. The whip which His followers must now use is a thorough understanding of what is at stake and of the manner in which this evil can be conquered.

The practice of usury has been condemned right back into Old Testament times, in Leviticus 25:36, 37; Exodus 22:25; Nehemiah 5:7-10; Psalm 15:5; Proverbs 28:8; Isaiah 24:2; Jeremiah 15:10; Ezekiel 18:8, 13, 17; also 22:12.

In the New Testament, Our Lord in the Sermon on the Mount, Luke 6:35, forbade the charging of interest on a loan.

The Greek philosophers also condemned usury. Patrick Cleary in The Church and Usury, page 26, states Plato said it sets the poor against the rich, describing usurers as despicable. Aristotle despised usury, and Cicero equated usury with murder.

The 2nd Lateran Council convened by Innocent II in 1139 denounced usury as did Innocent III in 1206. The penalty for usury was excommunication. Christians were not allowed to witness a usurer's will. Usurers' wills were invalid, and their chattels forfeit. The Council of Tours in 1163 further strengthened the clergy, decreeing the restitution of all monies by the descendants of usurers until all were repaid.

Under the leadership of Archbishop Langton and some Christian barons, Canon Law became the law of the land, and Magna Carta was signed at Runnymede, June 15, 1215. This forced King John to restrict taxation, guaranteed home ownership and property rights, so that today an Englishman's home is said to be his castle. Of the 63 clauses in Magna Carta, clauses 7 and 8 dealt with protecting the debtor and his heirs from Crown agents and Jews. (Encyclopedia Brittanica p. 577).

There followed a period of unprecedented prosperity. The English penny was the same value for 400 years. The average working man only worked 150 days a year and he enjoyed a far higher standard of living than he does today being fed a quart of beer and meat daily. It was during this period that all the beautiful cathedrals of Europe were built mostly by voluntary labor.

In 1835 Pope Benedict XIV issued the Encyclical *Vix Pervenit* which condemns usury in all of the old terms (Patrick Cleary, p. 160).

Had England remained faithful to Rome is it not likely that another Archbishop Langton would succeed in casting out the money lenders in defense of the common people as had been so successfully done at Runnymede in 1215?

Chapter 4

THE ROLE OF SECRET SOCIETIES

The question may be asked why should any society be secret, especially to the point of taking an oath to keep its secrets, if it has not something sinister to hide. For more than two centuries the Popes with good reason have written encyclical after encyclical condemning secret societies. They are a new and terrible phenomenon of which there is no complete parallel in any other period of history. In 1776 their declared aim was "Novus Ordo Saeculorum", a new world order. The main weapons to be used in the fulfillment of that aim were financial control and war. Financial control meant power as we have seen in the last chapter.

By moving nations towards war meant the quickest and most effective way to get those nations into their financial grasp. War was also chosen because it inevitably breaks down irreparably the level of morality, patriotism, industriousness, honorable personal ambition, dependence on close family relationships and a dozen other characteristics of our former civilization. Up to this time disparate groups everywhere had fancy notions about grabbing power for themselves for the time being.

In 1776 it was different. One Adam Weishaupt, a Bavarian professor, set out to obtain, in time, total control over the whole human race. He founded what is known as the Order of the Illuminati. To implement his great idea he planned and organized the French Revolution. This he accomplished by absorbing into his Order the Masonic Lodges of France. The Reign of Terror of that revolution will give some idea of the nature of Weishaupt's ambitions.

Eleven Popes have condemned those secret societies in terms so severe and so sweeping as to be quite unique in the history of the Church. The Popes were Clement XII, Benedict XIV, Pius VI, Pius VII, Leo XII, Pius VIII, Gregory XVI, Pius IX, Leo XIII, Pius X, Pius XI. In 1884, in the encyclical *Humanum Genus* Pope Leo XIII said to the bishops of the world: "Tear away the mask of Freemasonry (secret society) *and make plain to all what it is.* It aims at the utter overthrow of the whole religious order of the world which Christian teaching has produced, and the substitution of a new state of things -- based on the principles of pure naturalism. Including almost every nation in its grasp it unites itself with other sects of which it is the real inspiration and the hidden motive power. It first attracts and then retains its associates by the bait of worldly advantage which it secures for them. *It bends governments to its will, sometimes by promises, other times by threats.* It has found its way into every class of society and forms an invisible and irresponsible power, an independent government as it were within the body corporate of the lawful state. It denies that our first parents sinned, and consequently that man's free will is in any way weakened or inclined to evil.

Wherefore we see that men are publicly tempted by the many allurements of pleasure, that there are journals or pamphlets without moderation or shame, that stage plays are remarkable in license, that designs for works of art are shamelessly sought in the laws of so-called realism -- and that all the blandishments of pleasure are diligently sought out by which virtue may be lulled to sleep. There have been in these secret societies some who have proposed artfully and of set purpose, that the multitude should be satiated with a boundless license of vice, as when this had been done it could come more easily under their power and authority."

Communism is the child of those secret societies so roundly condemned by so many Popes. The Catholic world was at least well warned, but unfortunately Catholics hardly ever heard, or if they did, it was by chance, of such warnings. The social teaching of the Church is the great and only body of teaching that can combat the evils of the day. This is logical. If Christ said He would be with His Church all days till the end of time He could not have left His Church helpless in face of such evil opposition. What a tragedy that young Catholics are still coming out of Catholic schools not knowing, not what the social teaching of the Church contains, but not knowing that it even exists. But they know there is such a thing as Marxism-Leninism and many of them believe it has all the right answers to the social problems of the world. Our Lady at Fatima said that the sacrifice She asked was that people should fulfill the duties of their station in life. It is surely the duty of someone's station in life that our youth should not have to come out of school with their hands tied behind their backs for lack of knowledge of the evil ideas confronting the world today and with which they will have to grapple.

Pope Pius XI wrote: "There is another explanation for the rapid diffusion of the Communist ideas now seeping into every nation great and small, advanced and backward, so that no corner of the earth is free from them. The explanation is to be found in a propaganda so truly diabolical that the world perhaps never witnessed its like before. It is directed from one common centre. It is shrewdly adapted to the varying conditions of diverse peoples. It has at its disposal great financial resources, gigantic organizations, international congresses and countless trained workers. Little by little it penetrates all classes and even reaches the better-minded citizens of the community with the result that few are aware of the poison which increasingly pervades their minds and hearts. It is satan's army on earth. It is in a certain sense satan himself, the adversary of God and the children of God."

Pope Pius IX condemned those secret societies on six different occasions, applying to them the words of Our Lord "You are from your father, the devil, and it is the works of your father that you wish to do."

In his first encyclical St. Pius X said: "So extreme is the general perversion that there is room to fear, that we are experiencing the foretaste and beginnings of the evils which are to come at the end of time and that the son of perdition, the Anti-Christ, has already arrived on earth."

It is important to bear in mind that the Order formed by Weishaupt is the parent of all secret societies directing and inspiring all that they do.

Today there are two highly important offshoots, one called the Bilderbergers, now wearing a low profile since its chairman, Prince Bernhardt of the Netherlands, was discovered to have been involved in questionable financial deals. Far more important though is a group known as the Trilateral Commission. This Commission is so secretive when it meets there are usually 30 to 40 plainclothes security men on duty round the meeting place. Outside that again a large squad of the country's police are stationed. The press is not allowed to attend and no statement is made to the press. The subject matter of the discussions is supposed to be trade between Japan, the U.S., and Western Europe, but why the secrecy? It was founded by the Rockefeller family and only the VIPs from any country are invited to attend.

Senator Mary Robinson was a member of the Executive for a time, but resigned when it became an embarrassment to her when purporting to represent Labour in a Dáil election in the 1970's. Dr. Garrett Fitzgerald is also a member, how important only he can tell. The Trilateral Commission was made an issue in the last U.S. presidential election. Candidate Reagan promised that no member of the Trilaterals would enter his cabinet, but that was soon forgotten when the President discovered who was master in the

U.S. *Trilaterals over Washington, Parts I and II* by Professor Anthony Sutton, tells all that can be known from the outside about this most secret of secret societies. Of this we can be sure the secret societies are gaining ground all the time, and power. Total power over the whole human race is the objective.

Communism is the offspring of those secret societies condemned by so many Popes over two centuries. Renowned scholars now believe that the Communist conspiracy is the puppet conspiracy and that its masters hide within secret society inside secret society in concentric circles operating from the West.

In the last century the Irish Bishops condemned the secret societies operating in Ireland, and quite rightly. However they omitted to explain to the brave young men who had joined those societies (for no other purpose but to free Ireland from the domination of England) the evil purposes of such societies, and that they, the young men eager to free their country from a foreign yoke were only being used to initiate world revolution which was designed to end in the most ruthless world dictatorship.

When no such explanation was given to those brave young men they naturally took it for granted that the bishops were on the side of the British government and against freedom in their country. Many were excommunicated and lived out their lives in the most bitter feelings against the Church, all because they were totally unaware of any sinister international forces being instrumental in running their secret societies.

In the month of August 1879 a meeting of one such secret society was held in a public house in County Mayo. During the meeting the matter of the preaching against such societies by the then parish priest of Knock parish was discussed. It was felt that to shoot a priest would be going a bit too far, but that he should be taught a lesson. Accordingly two young men were ordered to cut off his ears on the following Saturday when he was to come to an out parish* to hear confessions.

The two young men were appalled at what they were commanded to do, but as to this very day, they were afraid to disobey an order. To do so often meant torture and death for the offending member. On this occasion Our Lady found a way out for the two young men under such satanic orders. On the Thursday before the fatal day a vision appeared on the wall of the little Church at Knock. The vision was of a live lamb standing on a table about the size and height of an altar. All around the altar Angels bowed in adoration. A little in front stood St. John holding a missal. This was so real a little boy jumped over the outside wall, (and) looked over the pages of the missal which fluttered slightly. Beside St. John stood Our Lady looking towards Heaven in ecstasy, and beside Her stood St. Joseph in silent prayer.

The vision lasted two hours and was witnessed by fifteen people of all ages. It rained heavily, the wind blowing towards the gable where the vision took place yet no rain touched the place of the vision.

* Note: An out parish; a rural parish having no resident pastor.

Like Lourdes and other shrines of Our Lady countless miracles of body, mind and soul have been taking place there ever since that day in August, 1879.

Immediately following the vision all fear of disobeying the order to cut off the priest's ears left the two young men. There was a general exodus from such a heinous society. Straight away Michael Davitt founded the Land League, an open society binding its members to neither oaths nor stringent rules. In a very short time the Land League did more for small tenant farmers than all the secret societies the country had ever known, so much so that today the Irish small farmer has greater security of tenure than his opposite number in any part of the world.

Students of the Insider/Conspiratorial theory of history insist that the idea of the 1916 Rising was hatched in the secret societies in Britain, though of course we don't have the minutes of their meetings! As always, it used idealistic and brave young men and women to carry out its plans. At the time Home Rule for Ireland, all Ireland, was on the British statute book. This then is what the Rising achieved for Britain. It was an excuse to shoot all our natural leaders, it was a further excuse to inflict on Ireland the bloody minded criminal Black and Tans, through the instrumentality of the Scottish Rite of Freemasonry, it achieved the division of our country with six counties torn away from the rest of the land. It created lasting enmity between the two religious sections within those six counties, and finally it has ended in the horrifying and frightful atrocities which have been taking place since 1968.

Remember the masterminds of those secret societies were and always have been internationalists, who never lose sight for a moment of total power for themselves through world government. To achieve this the breakup of the British Empire was necessary. The 1916 Rising was the inspiration of all the subject peoples of the British Empire to look for self government. Most of them little understood that they were to be freed from one kind of tyranny only to be saddled with something far worse, a Communist dictatorship. General Lowe, who commanded the British troops in Ireland in 1916 said he was never in doubt that the Rising could be put down in a week. Knowing this, how clever that all the officers should be away at the Fairyhouse Races, when the Rising began, giving the impression that they were taken by surprise.

Under Section 65 of the 1920 Government of Ireland Act, it was stipulated that all secret societies were to be outlawed with one exception, that of the Masonic Order. Do we wonder then that the immediate outcome of the Treaty was a Civil War and the assassination of Michael Collins? He knew too much about the workings of the secret societies and had intended that interest bearing government debt would never be part of our way of life. Today every PAYE taxpayer pays more than 80% of his taxes to service such debt, and he hasn't the faintest idea how he is being conned out of this money.

German Bishop Kettler, founder of Catholic Action wrote in 1865: "By general consent or conspiracy among European writers, freemasonry alone is regarded as a sacrosanct subject which no one must touch upon. Everybody fears to speak of it, as if it were a kind of evil spirit. This strange position of affairs is of itself a proof of the immense power which freemasonry exercises in the world."

In 1925 the Feast of Christ the King was instituted by Pius XI who wrote: "When once men recognize both in private and public life, that Christ is King, society will at last receive the great blessings of real liberty, well-ordered discipline, peace and harmony." But our enemy within the Church has done its job well, this great encyclical not alone is not being put into practice, it is not even in print. Pius XI continues: "We wish to speak to the rulers of nations. To you most of all is committed the responsibility of safeguarding the common good. You can contribute so much to the preservation of morals. We beg of you never to allow the morals of your peoples to be undermined. The family is the primary unit in the state. Do not tolerate any legislation which would introduce into the family those practices which are opposed to the Natural Law of God. For there are other ways by which a government can and should solve the problems of the family, that is to say by enacting laws which will assist families and by educating the people wisely, so that the Moral Law and the freedom of the citizens are both safeguarded."

Since the death of Bobby Sands on hunger strike the Provos are known the world over. They came into existence in 1970 in disgust that the main body to which they belonged had become Marxist-Leninist. This title is used in Ireland to conceal from the ordinary voter that Marxist-Leninist means Communist. The Provos initially saw it as their reason for existence to continue the struggle for a united Ireland and to protect the minority in the Six Counties who certainly needed protection at the time. Today one doesn't need to be clairvoyant to observe that members of the secret societies so much condemned by so many Popes have wormed their way into the Party and to the very top where they exercise control. In recent times many idealistic young men from north and south have joined from the noblest motives, but once inside, and not liking what they saw found there was no way out. Like the two young men in Knock parish in the last century they are afraid not to carry out orders no matter how repugnant such orders may be to them personally.

Once again the secret societies seem to be winning.

Cardinal Pie, Bishop of Poitier, mentor of Pope Pius IX on social issues, giant of Vatican I, wrote: "When a country's Christianity is reduced to the proportions of domestic life, when Christianity is no longer the soul of public life, of the power of the state and of public institutions, then Jesus Christ will treat such a country as He Himself is treated. He will continue to bestow His Grace and His Blessings on those who serve Him but He will abandon the institutions and authorities that do not serve Him, and such institutions, authorities, kings and races become like the sands of the desert or like the dead leaves in autumn which can be blown away by a gust of wind."

The following is an extract from Italian *Alta Vendita* (or *Haute Vente*) documents. These documents were seized by the Pontifical Government in 1846: "Let the clergy march under your banner in the belief that they are marching under the banner of the Apostolic Keys . . . Lay your nets in the depths of the sacristies, seminaries, and convents . . . Let us spread vice broadcast among the multitude; let them breathe it in through their five senses; let them drink it in, and become saturated with it. Make men's hearts corrupt and vicious, and you will no longer have Catholics. Draw away the priests from the altars and from the practice of virtue. Strive to fill their minds and occupy their time with other matters . . . it is the corruption of the masses we have undertaken -- *the corruption of the people through the clergy, and of the clergy by us* -- the corruption which ought one day to enable us to lay the Church in the tomb."

Chapter 5

THE ESSENCE OF COMMUNISM

Pope Pius XI described Communism as intrinsically evil. No Pope would ever make such a statement lightly. If then Communism is intrinsically evil it has got to be the antithesis of Christianity.

Christ, the Second Person of the Blessed Trinity, came on earth to save mankind. He said: "I am the Way, the Truth and the Life." He died for each one of us individually just as if each one of us was the only person in existence. To the Christian then, human life is sacred, counted above all the material things of this world, with which there never could be any comparison. The right to that life, from the moment of conception to the moment he draws his last breath, comes from God, the Creator of that life, and must never be taken away from him.

According to Communism all rights come from the state or the collective. The individuals count for nothing, and may be sacrificed in millions if necessary to suit the collective. The gullible will be told that in the collective everyone will have his say, that the collective is a democracy. How does this operate in practice? We have it on no less an authority than that of Trotsky himself that it works as follows: the Communist Party dictates to the proletariat: the central committee dictates to the Communist Party: the Politburo dictates to the central committee and finally the Secretary dictates to the Politburo. This Stalin did for thirty years. Thus we have one man, a dictator, deciding how not only the millions of people in his own country will live but how the millions in every country where Communism has got a foothold will live.

The claim of a right of control has been formalized in what is known as the Brezhnev Doctrine. This doctrine states that it is the responsibility of the international Communist movement to ensure that no Communist government is ever overthrown by the people of any country once it gets into power in that country, and if such overthrow appears imminent military intervention is imperative and moral (Communist morality). This ensures that once the dictatorship of the Communist Party has been imposed on any country it will remain there forever, barring miracles. Freedom comes out of the barrel of a gun as Hungary and Czechoslovakia discovered when they tried to shake off the Communist yoke. There is one miracle recorded. Ten per cent of the people of Austria were saying the Rosary that the Communists would leave their country and in 1955 they did. It was the only country the Communists ever left voluntarily or otherwise.

To the Christian the family is sacred. It is the basic unit of society. "For this a man shall leave father and mother, house and home and cleave to his wife, and they shall be two in one flesh, till death shall them part . . . What God has joined together let no man put asunder."

Communism claims that all rights come from the state, that marriage is a purely human contract, can be broken at will, and that the children belong to the state. Life in any Communist country, especially as it affects the family, has been classically described by George Orwell in *Animal Farm*. A child, any human being, is merely a thing, made to serve the almighty state.

Communism has declared war on three fundamental institutions, the family, religion (acknowledging God as the author of life) and on the ownership of private property.

Living Christianity would see the greatest possible number of people settled on, and owning the land on which they work. No man making a living on the good earth under his feet could ever be called a slave. Take away this most stable of all means of making a living, make the citizen dependent on an all-powerful state for food (through the ration book), clothes, shelter, light and water, then he is less free than the slaves of old. They at least knew their masters. The modern slave can look and wonder at the multi- storey office blocks whose inhabitants can be far more powerful and often far more menacing than standing armies.

Pius XI in his encyclical on Communism says: "But . . . ever since Adam's fall . . . virtue has had a bitter struggle to wage against vice . . . until we have come to the revolution of our time . . . threatening to reduce whole nations to a state of barbarism worse than that which prevailed among most peoples before the coming of the Redeemer . . . We are alluding to none other than Bolshevist Communism whose one aim is to upset completely the ordered structure of society and undermine the very foundations of Christian civilization . . . Our predecessors warned the world in plain terms what would be the outcome of thus divorcing human society from Christian principles . . ."

The false doctrines of Communism were also solemnly denounced as long ago as 1846 by Pius IX. He wrote in *Qui Pluribus* of "that infamous doctrine of Communism utterly opposed to the natural law itself, the adoption of which would completely destroy all men's rights, their property and fortune, and even human society itself." (Note that this was the year 1846, two years before the famous Manifesto was issued, which was commissioned by a group calling themselves "The League of Just Men" now the master conspirators who had been founded by Weishaupt, in 1776, and who ever since have been able to keep an ever more tightening grip on all secret societies and to force them to do their bidding. Marx's name was not appended to the Manifesto until 20 years later.)

Pius XI continues: "Leo XIII described these same aberrations as a deadly plague insidiously penetrating the very vitals of human society and threatening it with extinction."

Pius XI goes on referring to Leo XIII, "that it was with an intuitive power characteristic of his mind that he showed how the organized tendency of the masses towards atheism, occurring in an age of great technical progress, was the result of a philosophy which had long sought to set up a barrier between science and faith, and between human life and the Church . . .

"In 1924, on the return of our relief mission from Russia we denounced the false doctrines and methods of Communism in one encyclical after another . . . we have solemnly protested against the persecution of Christians in Russia, in Mexico and in Spain . . ."

Pius XI in dealing with the theory of Communism states: "The theory teaches that matter, with its blind and hidden forces, is the only reality which exists, and that it is matter which by a natural process evolves into a tree, an animal or a man. Even human society is only a particular manifestation or form of matter, evolving in the same way and tending by an irresistible necessity and by a perpetual conflict of forces to the attainment of its final goal, which is a classless society. Such a doctrine obviously leaves no room for the idea of an eternal God, for a distinction between spirit and matter, or between body and soul, for the survival of the soul after death, or for any hope of a future life . . .

"And because . . . the human person is nothing more than a cog in the machinery of the world system, they deny to individuals all the natural rights . . . and ascribe them to the community . . . even parental authority is repudiated, nor is any individual allowed the right of ownership over natural resources or the means of production. In a system which thus scorns and rejects all the sacred functions of human life, it follows as a matter of course that matrimony and the family are considered as a purely civil and artificial institution . . . and as a necessary consequence denies the indissoluble perpetuity of wedlock.

"The complete emancipation of woman from any ties with home and family is a special characteristic of the Communist theory. Held to be totally free from the protective authority of her husband, thrust into the turmoil of public life and communal industry, her home and children being handed over to the custody of the state . . . Parents finally are denied the right to educate their children . . .

"What does human society become, based on these materialistic principles? An association of human beings, with no other principle of unity save an authority deriving from economic factors. Its sole function is to produce wealth by communal labor, and its sole aim is the enjoyment of material goods in a paradise where each man gives labor according to his strength and receives wealth according to his needs.

"This system grants the state the right, indeed with unlimited and arbitrary power to direct individual citizens into communal industry regardless of their personal welfare, suitability or inclination, and even claims the right to direct the unwilling by force.

"Such is the doctrine . . . a doctrine full of error and sophistry, contrary to revelation and reason alike, a doctrine destructive of the foundations of civil society and subversive of social order, a doctrine which refuses to acknowledge the true origin of the state, its true nature and purpose, which repudiates and denies the rights, the dignity, and the freedom of the human person . . ."

Thus the Church has been condemning Communism, and warning the people of the world of the consequences of not heeding its warning, since 1846, two years before the Communist Manifesto was produced. What is scarcely known by one in a million is that Marx was commissioned to write the manifesto by a group of conspirators calling themselves by no less a title than "The League of Just Men". Marx was a paid hack writer. It was all of twenty years later before Marx's name was appended to the manifesto. This secret group tracing its origin back to the Illuminati, founded in Bavaria in 1776 had, and still has, one clear-cut objective, nothing less than world government which in essence could be nothing but a dictatorship. That dictatorship has already been established over a billion people who gaze beyond the Iron and Bamboo Curtains hoping and believing that their salvation will come from the so-called free West, some day, somehow, they just hope.

Gary Allen, author of the bestseller *None Dare Call It Conspiracy* which by 1972 had sold 7,000,000 copies in the U.S. has described this élite as pursuing an international conspiratorial drive for power by men in high places willing to use any means to bring about their desired aim, global conquest. In recent years this élite has become worried that their real aims will become known to a sufficient number of people to pose a threat to their designs, so they have renamed their ideal of global conquest as the New World Order.

Allen says that unless we understand the conspiratorial nature of Communism we cannot understand it at all. Dialectical materialism, Marxism-Leninism, etc., are merely the techniques used to keep people mesmerized and tied down. The visible Communists are merely the puppets being made to dance to the tune of their hidden Masters, the world's richest and most powerful men. Dr. Bella Dodd was head of the Communist Party in New York during the 1939-45 War. She tells how she received orders that if ever she had difficulty in receiving instructions from Moscow, she was to go to any one of three designated men who lived in the Waldorf Towers Hotel. They would tell her what to do. What puzzled Dr. Dodd was that not one of these men so far as she knew had anything whatever to do with the Communist Party, but whenever they did give an instruction it was never changed by Moscow. All three were exceedingly wealthy American businessmen. They would need to be to live in the Waldorf Towers.

Professor Carroll Quigley, possibly the world's most renowned historian, in his monumental book, *Tragedy and Hope*, describes this New World Order -- a nicer name than Communist dictatorship -- as "nothing less than to create a world system of financial control in *private* hands, able to dominate the political system of each country and the economy of the world as a whole . . . his, the individual's freedom and choice will be controlled within very narrow alternatives by the fact that he will be numbered from birth, and followed, as a number, through his educational training, his required military or other public service, his tax contributions, his health and medical requirements, and his final retirement and death benefits."

The network, as it is sometimes called, wants control over all natural resources, business, banking and transportation, by controlling the governments of the world. To bring this about nothing can compare with a good hot war, so the élite has had no qualms about fomenting wars, depressions where millions are unemployed, and a very important ingredient, hatred. They want a monopoly which would eliminate all competitors and destroy the free enterprise system. (John D. Rockefeller, Sr. is on record as saying that competition is a sin.)

There are two ways of eliminating competition. One has been described by Mao Tse-tung as freedom coming out of the barrel of a gun. The more cunning and crafty way, and possibly the more enduring way, is by legislation, which never fails to give itself high-sounding names, and which is generally dictated by the wheelers and dealers of international finance. By merger, take-over bid, by instilling fear of bankruptcy and myriads of other ways competition is being eliminated until eventually the favored few of the élite will control the whole world. In large measure they already do. They have deliberately manipulated the present inflation rate, back-breaking taxation system, and the massive unemployment which is leading to anarchy.

Christ fasted for forty days before commencing His public life. At the end of the forty days the devil took Him up into a high mountain and showed Him all the kingdoms of the earth, saying: "All these will

I give You, if You will bow down and adore me." As every Christian knows, Christ said: "Begone, satan." It does now look as if satan in recent history brought the élite, about which we are writing, up into a high mountain and showed them all the kingdoms of the earth, repeating what he had said to Our Lord, only this time the élite bowed down and took the devil's shilling or whatever one calls his symbol of power, and satan would appear to have made good his promises.

Christ was gentle, kind and forgiving to the greatest of sinners provided they repented, but there was a time when He was angry. He was so angry He made a whip and drove the money changers out of the Temple. Was it a symbolic action? The conspirators have now almost total power over the world's money supply. They can deflate or inflate as they wish. Either way they can bring about the same results, depression, millions unemployed, a world without hope. In the days when everything was made by hand, the Golden Age of Christianity, it was said that life should be a series of festivals, interspersed by work.

Where the machine can now do the work of fifty men, millions go in want in the midst of plenty. The power of the élite is almost absolute. According to Professor Quigley, this élite wants control over all natural resources, the production and distribution of goods and this in turn means control of people. Nationalize or communize everything in a country and you have your objective with the stroke of a pen.

The élite wants to centralize, centralize, centralize all decision-making so that at the top they will make all the decisions. The answer is to decentralize, decentralize, decentralize until the people in even the smallest locality have control over their own affairs. The Popes call this the principle of subsidiarity in their encyclicals.

Communism then being intrinsically evil, and condemned by Pope after Pope since 1846, could never be the answer to the many and complex social problems of the peoples of the world. "If, as claimed by humanism, (the Western brand of Marxism) man were born only to be happy, he would not be born to die. Since his body is doomed to death, his task on earth evidently must be more spiritual: not a total engrossment in everyday life, not the search for the best ways to obtain material goods and then their carefree consumption. It has to be the fulfillment of a permanent, earnest duty so that one's life's journey may become above all an experience of moral growth: to leave life a better human being than one started it. It is imperative to reappraise the scale of the usual human values: its present incorrectness is astounding. It is not possible that assessment . . . of performance should be reduced to the question of how much money one makes . . . Only by the voluntary nurturing in ourselves of freely accepted and serene self-restraint can mankind rise above the world stream of materialism." Solzhenitsyn at Harvard, 1978.

Chapter 6

THE TAKEOVER IN RUSSIA

"There is no proletarian, not even a communist movement that has not operated in the interests of money, in the direction indicated by money, and for the time being permitted by money -- and that without the idealists among the leaders having the slightest suspicion of the fact."

Oswald Spengler, in *The Decline of the West*

Many serious students of history maintain that the 1914-18 War was fought solely in order to obtain a geographical foothold for Communism in Russia. The supposed reason for the outbreak of that War was the assassination of a Crown Prince. Now if someone is killed, king or pauper, the course of justice is to pursue the killer and make him pay the penalty. Instead, in 1914 to 1918 fifty-five million people were killed, the sufferings of their relatives and friends can never be gauged, the flower of Europe's manhood was lost, all because one man was killed. It is preposterous to believe that this was the reason for the war. Early in 1917 it looked as if the war would end in stalemate, that there would be a negotiated peace, no one being declared the winner. But that was not allowed to be because then Communism could never have been established in Russia.

The key to foisting Communism on Russia was to get America into the war. This was a difficult job because ninety-nine per cent of the ordinary people of America wanted to have nothing to do with Europe or its wars.

In 1916 a Presidential election was fought in the U.S. Wilson, the winner, had one issue and one issue only. His script writers said: He will keep us out of the war in Europe, and of course he won with a resounding victory. What the ordinary voters did not know was that the stage was already well set for getting America into the war. The ruse used was the sinking of the Lusitania off the coast of Cork with the loss of many American lives. But the extraordinary thing was that the Lusitania had been sunk two years earlier. Before it sailed the Germans had taken full page advertisements in New York newspapers telling civilians not to travel on it, that it would contain arms, and was likely to be torpedoed. Nevertheless the ballyhoo worked and Americans against their will were catapulted into the European war to end all wars.

At the beginning of 1917 Trotsky was in New York. He was supposed to be a penniless journalist writing the odd article for some Communist newspaper. Yet Trotsky lived in a luxury flat, had a maid and a chauffeur. When he set out for Russia he brought with him a boatload of arms and 277 trained revolutionaries. All this was paid for by the Wall Street banking firm of Kuhn, Loeb & Co., in which the two brothers Warburg, natives of Berlin, were partners. Another partner was Jacob Schiff. According to Jacob's grandson, John Schiff, in the New York journal, *America,* of February 23rd, 1949, "Today it is estimated the old man sank about twenty million dollars for the final triumph of Bolshevism in Russia", so twenty million dollars of one man's private fortune went for the final triumph of Communism in Russia. (Quoted in Gary Allen's book *None Dare Call It Conspiracy*.)

While Trotsky was arranging all this in New York including the acquiring of an American passport after only a three months' stay there, where was Lenin? Lenin was in Switzerland. The two Warburg brothers who helped to finance Trotsky in New York had a brother in Berlin. In conjunction with the German High Command, this Warburg brother arranged to put Lenin into a sealed train, to give him eight million pounds in gold and to see that the train got all the way to Moscow unmolested, there to meet up with Trotsky and his menagerie. It should be noted that when Trotsky was passing by Nova Scotia on the SS Christiana with his arms, his revolutionaries, and his twenty million dollars, the coast guard arrested him, believing quite rightly that he was up to no good. Power is the name of the game. Trotsky didn't have to endure the rigors of a Canadian jail more than a few days. He managed to get busy on the phone. Where to, do you think? Naturally to Wall Street and believe it or not to Washington. (An ordinary citizen should try this sometime.) Amazing as it may seem Trotsky was allowed on his way on orders from no less a person than President Wilson himself.

It should be noted that Jacob Schiff's daughter was married to one of the Warburg brothers named Felix. He and his brother Paul came to New York from Berlin at the turn of the century, and joined the firm of Kuhn, Loeb & Co. Max remained in Berlin where he was also in the banking business.

We now see that Communism was foisted on the unfortunate Russian people by money, vast sums of it, and thorough organization extending far and wide. A White Russian General named Arsene de Goulevitch, in his book *Czarism and the Revolution*, has this to say: "The main purveyors of funds for the revolution, however, were neither the crackpot Russian millionaires nor the armed bandits of Lenin. The 'real' money primarily came from certain British and American circles which for a long time past had lent their support to the Russian revolutionary cause . . .

The important part played by the wealthy American banker, Jacob Schiff, in the events in Russia, though as yet only partially revealed is no longer a secret . . . On April 7, 1917, General Janin made the following entry in his diary ('Au GCC Russe' -- At Russian GHQ -- *Le Monde Slave*, Vol. 2, 1927, pp. 296-7): 'Long interview with R. who confirmed what I had previously been told by M. After referring to the German hatred of himself and his family, he turned to the subject of the Revolution which, he claimed, was engineered by the English and, more precisely, by Sir George Buchanan and Lord (Alfred) Milner. Petrograd at the time was teeming with English . . . He could, he asserted, name the streets and the numbers of the houses in which British agents were quartered. They were reported, during the Rising, to have distributed money to the soldiers and incited them to mutiny . . . In private interviews I have been told that over twenty-one million rubles were spent by Lord Milner in financing the Russian Revolution."

In passing it is well to note that the Paris Peace Conference which laid so well the plans for the 1939-45 war had representing 'their' respective countries none other than Lord Milner, and all three Warburg brothers, Paul, Felix and Max who had so heavily financed both Trotsky and Lenin. These millionaires were able to provide the money and the organization without which no revolution can be successful. Where would the so-called downtrodden masses find such millions and the sophisticated expertise in organization. The super-rich could provide both. The reader may ask, but why? Why would the super-rich hand guns to those who vow to shoot them in their beds? Another point to remember is that the revolution would have petered out in a few months if it were not for the massive financial and other aid which came from the same super rich coterie.

In the 1920's these same people poured millions of dollars and pounds into saving what Lenin called his New Economic Program, thus saving the Soviets from collapse. Why would the super-rich, men like the Rothschilds, Rockefellers, Schiffs, Warburgs, Harrimans and Milners want to save the Soviets, whose avowed aim, they shout from the housetops, is to divest all these rich men of their wealth and share it out to each according to his needs? Obviously, if such men have set up Communism and given it its first geographical foothold in Russia they are not afraid of anything Communism can do to them, and that they in fact control its every move. As Gary Allen commented, although it was not their main purpose, by nationalization of Russia the rich men, or "Insiders" as they are known, bought themselves an enormous piece of real estate, complete with mineral rights for somewhere between thirty and forty million dollars.

One can only theorize on the manner in which control is exercised. Professor Anthony Sutton of the Hoover Institute of War and Peace has written a number of books on the subject, having spent more than twenty years examining government documents and other unimpeachable material relating to the economic aid being sent by the West to the Soviets.

One of the most revealing descriptions of the motivation of those who destroyed Imperial Russia and promoted Communism is provided in a remarkable book, *Geneva versus Peace*, by Comte de Saint-Aulaire, French Ambassador to Great Britain from 1920 to 1924 (Sheed and Ward, London, 1937). The French Ambassador records a dinner comment by a Jewish revolutionary involved in the short-lived Bela Kun Communist régime in Hungary after the First World War. The revolutionary had subsequently become a director of "a great New York bank, one of those which were financing the Bolshevik Revolution". When a fellow guest asked him "how it was possible for high finance to protect Bolshevism," he replied, " 'Too much salt corrodes meat, too little lets it rot.'

The precept can with justice be applied both to the human mind and to the peoples of the earth. We, Jews, apply it wisely as it should be applied, salt being the emblem of wisdom. We mingle it discreetly with the bread that men consume. We administer it in corrosive doses only in exceptional cases, when it is necessary to get rid of the *debris* of an immoral past, as in the case of Czarist Russia. That gives you a partial explanation why Bolshevism finds favor in our eyes; it is an admirable salting tub in which to corrode and destroy and not to preserve.

But beyond and above this particular instance we are in communion with Marxism in its purest form in the International, in other words with our religion, because it is the weapon of our nationalism, in turn defensive and offensive, buckler and sword. You will say that Marxism is the very antithesis of capitalism which is equally sacred to us. It is precisely for this reason that they are direct opposites to one another, that they put into our hands the two poles of this planet and allow us to be its axis. These two contraries, like Bolshevism and ourselves, find their identity in the International.

"In the management of the new world . . . our organization for revolution is evidenced by destructive Bolshevism and for construction by the creation of the League of Nations which is also our work."

Professor Sutton has written a three-volume history called *Western Technology and Soviet Economic Development*, wherein he proves beyond yea or nay that the USSR was actually built in the U.S.A. Because Sutton's arguments cannot be refuted he is ignored by the media which is of course the mouth-piece of these same rich men who have built the USSR into the military power that she now is. Professor Sutton has written two further books: *Wall Street and the Bolshevik Revolution* and *Wall Street and the Rise of Hitler*. Needless to say such books are not reviewed in the best places. In fact they are not reviewed at all. Sutton is just treated as if he never existed. With newspapers at all times so greedy for scoops how is it some bright reporter has never managed to ask the right questions and to get the answers into print? True, Sutton and other courageous writers on the conspiracy do get their books published by equally courageous publishers, but the rich men see to it that not one in a hundred people will ever hear of them, and one in a hundred will never manage to get his message to the ninety-nine.

Sutton's book *Wall Street and the Rise of Hitler* proves to the hilt that these same rich men set up Hitler to ensure that World War Two would take place on schedule. The purpose of World War Two was to extend the Communist yoke into Eastern Europe, which it did very successfully, and to China. However we hope to devote a special chapter to the handing over of China to the Communists by power-ful agents of the same men set up in the highest places of the U.S. government.

Professor Sutton proves that World War II was not only well planned, it was extremely profitable -- for a select group of financial insiders. Carefully tracing this closely guarded secret through original documents and eyewitness accounts, Sutton documents the roles played by J.P. Morgan, T.W. Lamont, the Rockefeller interests, General Electric Company, Standard Oil, First National City Bank, Chase and Manhattan banks, and of course Kuhn, Loeb & Co. and scores of other business élitists. On the cover of *Wall Street and the Rise of Hitler* it says this book shows how the bloodiest, most destructive war in history was financed and promoted. It is sure to spark angry denials and heated debate. But the publishers were not quite right. The book got the silent treatment, far more effective than denials and heated debate.

On page 111, in the chapter entitled, "Who Financed Hitler?", Sutton asks the question: How can we prove that these political payments actually took place? He then gives details of the bank through which the payments were made. He says: "There exists among the Nuremberg Trial papers the original transfer slips from the banking division of I.G. Farben and other firms listed on page 110 to the Delbruck Schickler Bank in Berlin, informing the bank of the transfer of funds from Dresdner Bank, and other banks, to their Nationale Treuhand (national trusteeship) account. This account was disbursed by Rudolph Hess for Nazi Party expenses during the election. Translation of the I.G. Farben transfer slip, selected as a sample, is as follows:

Translation of I.G. Farben letter of February 27, 1933, advising of transfer of 400,000 Reichsmarks to National Trusteeship account:

        I.G. Farbenindustrie Aktiengesellschaft

Bank Department

Firm Delbruckler & Co.
Berlin W.8   Mauerstrasse 63/65,
Frankfurt (Main) 20
Our ref: (Mention in reply) B/Goe
27 February 1933

We are informing you herewith that we have authorized
the Dresdner Bank in Frankfurt/M. to pay you tomorrow
forenoon RM400,000 which you will use in favor of the
account "Nationale Treuhand" (National Trusteeship).

Respectfully,
I.G. Farbenindustrie Aktiengesellschaft
by order
 (Signed) Selck   (Signed) Bangert
By special delivery

On page 126 Sutton states: "When we examine the
names comprising both the original pre-1933 Keppler
circle and the post-1933 expanded Keppler and Himmler circle, we find the Wall Street multi-nationals
heavily represented -- more so than any other institu-
tional group. Let us take each Wall Street multi-national
or its German associate in turn -- those identified in
chapter 7 as linked to financing Hitler -- and examine
their links to Keppler and Heinrich Himmler."

Sutton proves without a shadow of doubt that
Hitler was set up to make war in much the same way
as a match would be arranged between Cassius Clay
(Mohammed Ali) and some worthy opponent able to
give him a good fight.

There is one thing the conspirators or insiders dread, that is exposure. The power at their disposal is vast, apparently limitless. Every ounce of it that can be used is used to leave in the minds of the ordinary people of the world a very fixed idea that everything that is happening in the world is accidental, that it just can't be helped.

We are told that prostitution is the oldest profession in the world, but the poor unfortunate women who sell their bodies are often more sinned against than sinning. There is another form of prostitution. It is that of the universities, the intellectuals, the publishers, the media generally. All can live in far more comfort than any rich man's mistress if they go along with what is considered the right line. There was a sub-editor in the *New York Times* who stuck it out for thirty years. When he could take no more he resigned his job and wrote a book which he called *All the News that Fits*.

The *New York Times* had played a major role in handing Cuba over to the Communists. Day in, day out, in season and out of season, it kept up the chant that Castro was not a Communist. He was an idealist, just an agrarian reformer. The moment Castro got to power he announced that he was then and always had been a Communist. Fancy the *New York Times* not knowing.

Whittaker Chambers says in his book *Witness* that when he was editor of the Communist newspaper in New York, a young sub-editor in training was advised always to read the *New York Times*. There he would get the line to follow.

The world today has the appearance of one vast brothel where all but the few have their price. If those who could have spoken out, did, there would have been no First World War and no takeover by the Communists in Russia, or anywhere else. The Popes were warning the world since 1846 and long before, in encyclical after encyclical of what the secret societies were up to. Did even one Roman Catholic in a hundred know that such encyclicals existed, let alone know what they contained?

Even the clergy and Catholic teachers have never had the faintest idea what those encyclicals contained. Could not the Catholic Church have brought together a band of young people more dedicated than any Communist cadres, young people who would have the absolute assurance that they were preaching the word of God. Could it be that the insiders or conspirators wormed their way into the Church for the sole purpose of seeing that the fine body of social teaching enshrined in the encyclicals would lie buried?

Chapter 7

LIVING UNDER COMMUNISM

"Harvard's motto is 'Veritas". Many of you
have already found out and others will find
out in the course of their lives that truth
eludes us as soon as our concentration
begins to flag, all the while leaving the
illusion that we are continuing to pursue it.
This is the source of much discord. Also,
truth seldom is sweet, it is almost invariably
bitter."

Solzhenitsyn at Harvard, June 1978

John Noble, an American citizen, spent nine years
in various slave labor camps under the Communists.
He gives an account of his experiences in his book *I
was a Slave in Russia*, published by the Cicero Bible
Press, Broadview, Illinois. On page 43 he says: "I
realized once again that death was the least thing to
fear under the conditions of captivity by the Reds."
He says of those who ministered to the spiritual wants
of the prisoners: "Rising above the squalor and even
degeneracy of Muhlberg was the dedication of two
groups of men, the clergy and the physicians. The
Catholic priests and Protestant ministers did far more
than attend, under greatest difficulties, to their proper
churchly duties -- Masses said quickly in the corner

of a barracks, a sermon preached and a hymn softly sung behind the latrines. The priests and ministers performed their greatest work, I think (for those who had not become oblivious, rutting, feeding animals), by their humility. No job was too mean for them. To the humility of each job, whether amid the filth of the latrines or the mud outdoors, these men brought the sure and tremendous dignity of their faith."

Describing the cells in one of his many prisons he says: "The cell measured six by three feet, the size of a closet. A cot took up almost all the floor space. The walls were a dead white, and outside the door a 400 watt bulb glared day and night until the white of the walls seemed to seep through every part of my brain . . . Between the walls of each two cells there was a metal slot in which wood or coal fires could be built to heat the cells. Fires were got going in the slot about seven in the morning. By noon the walls were too hot to get near, and I gasped in the humid heat, wet with perspiration. In the evening the fires were permitted to go out, and the outer doors to the cell corridors were opened to let the freezing winds whip through. We had no blankets. Each night was a chattering, freezing night . . . Buchenwald had been branded as a virtual Nazi abattoir, yet, from prisoners who had been in the camp under both the Nazis and the Communists, I heard repeatedly that things were even worse now (under the Communists)."

Noble was moved from Buchenwald to Weimar where, after three years of no charge being preferred against him, he was finally told he had been sentenced to 15 years in a slave labor camp, which happened to be the Gulag. In all those years he never saw a solicitor, never had a charge preferred against him. He describes his sentence thus: "A girl at the table asked the inevitable, routine questions of identity and then shoved a printed form toward me. It had been filled in at two places. First there was my name. Then there was a space with the figure 15 written in. 'What is this?' I asked, pointing to the figure. 'You have been tried in Moscow and sentenced to 15 years of slave labor.' The paper read: 'Physical labor.'

'Why, for what reason, on what charge?' I blurted out.

'If there are any questions,' the girl replied curtly, 'ask them where you will be sent.' "

In all the years Noble spent in Communist camps he was never allowed to send even one postcard, or even one letter, and was never allowed to receive one. I now give a short excerpt of his description of the prison train to the Gulag, a journey which lasted six weeks: "I was jammed between other prisoners, feet hard against the train wall, hands at side, chin against the rough board of the shelf. There was no way to change positions, to arch one's back, to do anything. Twice a day we were taken to the bathroom. At other times, prisoners who could not hold themselves would whimperingly foul their pants and often also the prisoners next to them. Even in the community of hardship it was difficult for some prisoners not to hate the unfortunates who did this."

Noble worked at the Vorkuta Mines where a strike was organized once word got there that the East Germans were in revolt. At Vorkuta the prisoners heard that uprisings were taking place through the 20 million Gulag slave region. The strike lasted in all about ten days. Then many thousands were lured into a field where they were given to understand there would be negotiations concerning the settlement of the strike. When they were all assembled the Red soldiers turned the machine guns on them. That ended the strike. Forthwith the rest returned to work. Noble says: "My life in Vorkuta was the closest thing possible to a living death. It was a gruelling combination of slow but continuous starvation, exhausting work, killing cold, and abject monotony that destroyed many a healthier man than I."

Noble describes some of the tortures he saw. What I am about to set down here are by no means the worst. He says: "I helped to carry one of the beaten prisoners to his cell. He had been whipped with his shirt on. His skin was laid open from the ridge of his shoulders all the way to his belt line, and the shirt had been ground into the raw meat of his back. For an hour, with the doctor who was also a prisoner, I picked bits of shredded cloth from the wounds, trying always to pick bloody cloth rather than the slivers of split red flesh. When we had finished cleaning his back, we wrapped him in strips of toilet paper, the prison dispensary's gesture toward providing medicine for the man . . . More complex and subtle was the torture of the disinfecting cabinet. This was a large boilerlike metal cabinet in which mattresses had been disinfected but no longer used for the purpose. Prisoners could see this looming presence, with its high pressure steam pipes and valves. What they did not know, if they were new . . . was that the tank was no longer connected to receive steam. It was these new prisoners that went to the tank for their torture.

A prisoner was thrown into the tank by guards who were purposefully rough to intimate that severe punishment was under way. Inside, the terrified prisoner watched the steel hatch swing shut and heard the booming clang as the locking mechanism turned and the bolts seated themselves in their slots. In the total interior darkness, the prisoner could only expect a searing jet of steam or a choking cloud of poisonous gas to be pumped in. And so he would be left for a full day or two, the door never being opened.

After this ordeal, several prisoners were taken from the tank completely mad. No person ever emerged without serious nervous consequences. Most came out of it with hair turned gray. All were willing to confess to whatever the Communists wished them to confess." As well as being tortured, people were killed for what appeared to be no particular reason. The Russians killed because, almost literally, a number had been drawn from a hat, because some meaningless document in some meaningless proceedings had said to snuff out the candle.

The reasons for the killings were as remote and irrelevant to the Russian guards as was the concept of death itself. Their joking though, was not forced. Life had to end for certain integers in the state table of statistics. The process of execution, about which the guards sometimes boasted because it was so 'humane' was simplicity itself. After a condemned prisoner had undressed, he was led to a partly shattered wing of the prison. As he rounded the corner into a corridor a guard shot him in the back of the head. As each prisoner was shot, his body was dragged to the end of the corridor. By the end of a day's killing, a stack of sprawling bodies, naked or in undershirts, lay in the dark and dirty hall. A guard doused the bodies with gasoline and tossed on a match. The flames from the pyre made a light that often was seen by prisoners in other parts of the building. If questioned, a guard would explain that trash was being burned.

William C. Bullitt was America's first Ambassador to the USSR. In *A Talk with Voroshilov* he relates the following episode which occurred in the early reign of the Communists in the USSR. At a banquet in Russia in 1934, Voroshilov told Bullitt that in 1919 he persuaded eleven thousand Czarist officers at Kiev to surrender by promising them that if they surrendered they, their wives and their families would be permitted to return to their homes.

When they surrendered, he executed the eleven thousand officers and all male children, and sent the wives and daughters into the brothels for the use of the Russian Army. He mentioned in passing that the treatment they received in the brothels was such that none of them lived for more than three months. Voroshilov believed that in carrying out a crime of such staggering proportions he was merely being a good Marxist-Leninist. Has Marxism-Leninism mellowed, as some would have us believe? Nikita Krushchev is on record as saying "Anyone who thinks we have forsaken Marxism-Leninism deceives himself. That won't happen till shrimps learn to whistle."

Krushchev described Stalin as he condemned him. His description depicted a man so vile that most folk took it for condemnation. What he said, in effect, was this: Stalin was a murderer, he was not a reluctant murderer but an enthusiastic one. He enjoyed murder. He got a thrill out of the torture of his own friends. When the Jewish doctors were arrested and accused of poisoning Zhdanov, Stalin called in the man responsible for examining them and indicated the type of torture to be given each one. He gave three fundamental rules for getting confessions: "Beat, beat, and beat again." He said: "If you don't get a confession by this date, we will shorten you by a head."

Krushchev indicated that Stalin was a stark, raving madman: "When you went in to see him in the morning, he would look at you and say: 'What have you been up to? You have a shifty look in your eye today.' You never knew whether you would leave as his friend or under armed guard to be shot." He presents a picture of a murderer of limitless appetite, a picture of megalomaniacal, sadistic madness. But he concludes by saying: " Don't misunderstand me, Stalin was a good man. He was a Marxist-Leninist. He did these things as a good Marxist-Leninist."

Richard Wurmbrand, a Rumanian Baptist pastor spent 14 years in jail under the Communists. In his book *Tortured for Christ* he says:

"Beginning on August 23, 1944, one million Russians entered Rumania, and soon after the Com-

111

munists came to power. *It was not without the co-operation of the American and British rulers of that time* . . . The tragedy of all the captive nations is a responsibility on the hearts of American and British Christians . . . they must know they have assisted the Russians in imposing upon us a regime of murder and terror . . . The Communists convened a congress of all Christian bodies in our parliament building. There were four thousand priests, pastors and ministers of all denominations. These four thousand chose Josef Stalin as honorary president of the congress declaring that Communism and Christianity are fundamentally the same, and could co-exist. One minister after another said words of praise towards Communism and assured the new government of the loyalty of the Church . . . My wife sat near me and told me 'Richard, stand up and wash away this shame from the face of Christ.' I arose and spoke, praising not the murderers of Christians, but Christ and God, and said that our loyalty is due first to Him. Afterwards I had to pay for this.

"I will never forget my first encounter with a Russian prisoner. He told me that he was an engineer . . . When I asked him if he believed in God, he lifted towards me eyes without understanding and said: 'I have no such military order to believe. If I have an order I will believe.' . . . Here stood before me a man whose mind was dead, a man who had lost the greatest gift to mankind -- to be an individual. He could not think any more on his own . . . a typical Russian after all those years of Communist domination . . . The Communists took away everything from everybody.

From the farmer they took fields and sheep. From a barber or tailor they took his little shop. Very poor men suffered much.

"On Sunday, February 19th, 1948, I was kidnapped by the secret police . . . For over eight years no one knew if I was alive or dead. My wife was visited by secret police who posed as fellow prisoners. They told her they had attended my funeral. She was heart-broken.

"Tortures were sometimes horrible. I prefer not to speak too much about those through which I have passed . . . In another book *In God's Underground* I recount with many details all our experiences with God in jail.

"A pastor was tortured with red hot iron pokers and with knives. He was beaten very badly. Then starving rats were driven into his cell through a large pipe. He could not sleep . . . If he rested a moment the rats would attack him. He was forced to stand for two weeks, day and night. They wished to compel him to betray his brethren, but he resisted steadfastly. In the end, they brought his fourteen-year-old son and began to whip the boy in front of the father, saying that they would continue to beat him until the pastor said what they wished him to say . . . When he could not stand it any more, he cried to his son: 'I must say what they want. I can't bear your beating any more.' The son answered, 'Father, don't do me the injustice to have a traitor as parent . . . If they kill me, I will die with the words, Jesus and my fatherland.' The Communists, enraged, fell upon the child and beat him to death.

"Handcuffs were put on our wrists which had sharp nails on the insides. If we were totally still, they didn't cut us. But in bitterly cold cells, when we shook with cold, our wrists would be torn with the nails.

"Christians were hung upside down on ropes and beaten so severely that their bodies swung back and forth under the blows. Christians were put in ice-boxes, refrigeration cells, which were so cold, frost and ice covered the inside. I myself was thrown in one with very little clothing on. Prison doctors would watch through an opening until they saw symptoms of freezing to death. Then they would give a warning and guards would rush in and take us out and make us warm. When finally warmed, we would be put back in the ice-box to freeze -- over and over again. It continued endlessly. Even today I can't bear to open a refrigerator.

"We were put in wooden boxes only slightly larger than we were. This left no room to move. Dozens of sharp nails were driven into every side of the box with their razor-sharp points sticking into the box. While we stood perfectly still, it was all right. We were forced to stand in these boxes for endless hours. When we swayed with tiredness the nails would go into our bodies. If we moved or twitched a muscle there were the horrible nails.

"What Communists have done to Christians, sur-passes any possibility of human understanding. I have seen Communists torturing Christians and the faces of the torturers shone with rapturous joy. They cried out while torturing the Christians: 'We are the devil.'

"We wrestle not against flesh and blood, but against the principalities and powers of evil. We say that Communism is not from men but from the devil. It is a spiritual force -- a force of evil -- and can only be countered by a greater spiritual force, the Spirit of God.

"I heard one torturer say: 'I thank God, in whom I don't believe, that I have lived to this hour when I can express all the evil in my heart.' He expressed it in unbelievable brutality and torture on prisoners.

"I have testified before the Internal Security Sub-committee of the U.S. Senate. There I described awful things, such as Christians tied to crosses for four days and nights. The crosses were put on the floor and hundreds of prisoners had to fulfill their bodily necessities over the faces and bodies of the crucified ones. Then the crosses were erected again and the Communists jeered and mocked: 'Look at your Christ. How beautiful He is.'

I described how, after being driven nearly insane with tortures, a priest in the prison of Pitesti was forced to consecrate human excrements and urine and give Holy Communion to Christians in this form . . . All the Biblical descriptions of hell and the pains of Dante's Inferno are nothing in comparison with the tortures in Communist prisons.

"This is only a very small part of what happened on one Sunday and on many other Sundays in the prison of Pitesti. Other things simply cannot be said. My heart would fail if I should tell them again and again. They are too terrible and obscene to put in writing. That is what your brothers in Christ went through and go through *NOW*. One of our workers was a young girl of the Underground Church. The police discovered that she spread gospels and taught children about Christ. They decided to arrest her. To make the arrest more agonizing and painful they decided to delay the arrest until the very day she was to be married. When the bride saw the secret police she held out her hands to be handcuffed, looked towards her beloved, then kissed the chains and said: 'I thank my heavenly Bridegroom for this the jewel He has presented to me on my marriage day. I thank Him that I am worthy to suffer for Him.' She was dragged off with weeping Christians and a weeping bridegroom left behind. They knew what happens to young Christian girls in the hands of Communist guards. After five years she was released -- a destroyed, broken woman, looking thirty years older. Her bridegroom had waited for her . . .

"The tortures and brutality continued without interruption. When I lost consciousness or became too dazed to give the torturers any further hopes of confessions, I would be returned to my cell. There I would lie, untended and half dead to regain a little strength so they could work on me again. Many died at this point. In the ensuing years, in several different prisons, they broke four vertabrae in my back, and many other bones. They carved me in a dozen places. They burned and cut 18 holes in my body. Doctors in Oslo, seeing all this and the scars of the lung tuberculosis which I also had, have declared that my being alive today is a pure miracle. According to their medical books I should have been dead for years . . .

116

I believe God performed this wonder so that you could hear my voice crying out on behalf of the Underground Church behind the Iron Curtain. He allowed one to come out alive and cry aloud the message from your suffering, faithful brethren."

The mathematician Igor Shafarevitch, a member of the Soviet Academy of Science, has written a brilliantly argued book entitled *Socialism*; this is a penetrating historical analysis, in the opinion of Solzhenitsyn, demonstrating that socialism of any type and shade leads to a total destruction of the human spirit and to a levelling of mankind to death. His book was published in France in 1976.

Socialism is the royal road to Communism. In the October, 1921 issue of the English *Labour Monthly*, Shaw wrote that "compulsory labour, with death as the final penalty . . . is the keystone of socialism."

Chapter 8

HANDING CHINA OVER TO THE COMMUNISTS

The ordinary person when told that 200 million Russians were handed over to Communist tyranny, the greatest tyranny known in history, by a small group of the world's richest men as a stepping stone towards owning and controlling the whole world, which they now euphemistically call the New World Order, would regard such a story as too fantastic to believe. Against it would revolt the average man's inherent goodwill and desire to live and let live. But if the handing over of Russia to the Communist tyranny seems incredible, the manner in which China was handed to the top conspirators, whose pawns the Communists are, boggles the mind of anyone trying to fit the pieces into the jigsaw puzzle of world politics.

There are now many books written on the subject, the records are all there, the world's most renowned scholars have examined them, there can't be and is no denial of what happened, but as in the case of Russia the ordinary person just doesn't know what happened. He has been fed the kind of line that suits the insiders or conspirators who mostly own and control the media. If the "met" officer (the weatherman) tells you at night the morrow is going to be fine, you accept what he says because you regard him as an authority.

In the same way the man in the street accepts what the media says is happening in the world and why. Of course, he accepts that there are bad people in the world and that one set of bad people is just about as bad as the other, but the control at the top and from the top, this is something of which the man in the street is totally ignorant. How is he to know unless someone tells him? The man who has never studied algebra doesn't know what algebra is all about, through no fault of his own. We read of the man riding in the chariot reading scripture who said how can I know what it means unless someone tells me. How six hundred million Chinese were handed over to Communist tyranny is the story that follows. Naturally in an account of this kind, only the barest bones of the story can be given but any reader interested in the freedom of the human race from total global Communist tyranny would do well to read some of the many fine books written on the subject.

The insiders like nothing better than a good hot war. A state of war gives them almost carte blanche to go about their satanic business of moving much faster than they might otherwise manage towards total world domination, or what sounds so much nicer to the ear, the New World Order.

The 1914-18 war was fought successfully to give Communism a geographical foothold in Russia. The 1939-45 war was fought to extend that tyranny to Eastern Europe and China.

The war in Europe was over in reality in 1944, one full year before it was formally declared over. The German High Command was suing for peace through their ambassador in Turkey, adding that the Allies could leave Hitler to them. The German High Command would deal with him. This of course had to be very secretly done and word was only sent to Roosevelt. Roosevelt, if he ever opened his mouth about the move did so only to his immediate bosses, the insiders. It is recounted by a most patriotic American, Curtis Dall, who happens to be Roosevelt's only son-in-law, in a book called *FDR*, *My Exploited Father-in-Law*.

The American generals commanding in Europe at the time, 1944, wanted to move into Czechoslovakia and on to Berlin, which they could have easily done in 1944, but they were prevented by Eisenhower, another top insider, or perhaps, like Roosevelt, a top agent for the insiders. Naturally, the German generals heard nothing of the move for peace by the German High Command.

In speaking of Eisenhower it is well to mention here that he was personally responsible for a crime for which the West must ever hang its head in shame. I refer to the sending back into Stalin's arms of two million refugees, some of whom had left Russia at the very start of the Revolution. The question of what to do with refugees came up at Potsdam and Yalta, but it was explicitly agreed by Stalin, Churchill and Roosevelt that there would be no forced repatriation.

In spite of this solemn commitment, on Eisenhower's orders no less than two million refugees were forced into cattle trucks and such like at bayonet point and sent back to Russia. Many jumped into the sea or committed suicide any way they could rather than face what they knew to be their certain fate, the Gulag Archipelago. This is now fully documented by Professor Julius Epstein in his book *Operation Keelhaul*, published by the Devin-Adair Company, Old Greenwich, U.S.A.

Just as it was possible for the American army to reach Berlin and all of Eastern Europe by 1944, it could also have moved into Poland and all of Eastern Germany. However, if the war was fought to foist Communism on all those countries, the American armies had to be stopped and kept in their place. Arthur Bliss Lane was the American Ambassador to Poland in 1945. He saw at first hand all the moves to ensure that only a Communist government would rule in Poland. (Remember the war was supposed to have begun for the freedom of Poland). Ambassador Lane sent communiqué after communiqué back to Washington telling what was happening and urging the Allies, the U.S., Britain and France to intervene to save Poland. When he realized that his communiqués were being treated as if they had never been sent, he resigned his prestigious job, went back to the U.S., and wrote a book called *I Saw Poland Betrayed*.

Like all the other fine books that brave men wrote at the time to warn people of what was happening all round them to ensure their future enslavement, the book got the silent treatment, the deadly silence that would ensure that if there were people anywhere powerful enough to do something about the situation they would be in no danger of finding out the awful truth. So the freedom of the Poles about which a terrible war was now drawing to a close was left to the tender mercies of Stalin. As was remarked about the so-called peace treaty at the end of the 1914-18 war, it was not a peace treaty. It was merely a break in hostilities.

In 1916 the American people had voted overwhelmingly for President Wilson on his solemn undertaking to keep the American people out of the war. It was the main issue. He could do the job better than his opponent, or so the American people believed. Well, they were tricked. To get the American people into the second World War to end all wars required a degree of subtlety unmatched in history. Yet it was accomplished. In spite of the overwhelming antipathy of the American people to any involvement in the war, they were tricked yet again in 1941. Rather to be more precise the Japanese were the ones who were really tricked. Somehow they had to be made to attack, and it was made doubly sure that ships were so tightly packed together in Pearl Harbor that the maximum number of American lives would be lost. President Roosevelt got to grips with Japan over its occupation of Manchuria, giving Japan an ultimatum to evacuate the country or else. Tensions got high. At their height the Crown Prince of Japan offered to come to Washington to discuss the whole question. Washington would have none of such an offer. Pressures were kept being piled up on the Japanese, and then finally they fell into the trap and attacked Pearl

Harbor, which was what Roosevelt and his bosses wanted all along.

Washington pretended to be surprised despite the fact that the Americans had broken the Japanese code days before the attack and knew the hour and minute it would happen. Despite having a direct line to Pearl Harbor, the authorities there were not informed until the attack had already taken place, and then by ordinary wire service. Of course there was a sham enquiry and a scapegoat ready made. All this is now generally known in the U.S., but a new generation has grown up which has been brainwashed into thinking, well, it was just one of those things that happen anyway.

The war between the U.S. and Japan got under way. In Europe the U.S. fought the Germans as an ally of Russia, but in Asia the U.S. fought Japan practically alone. She did get some aid from Britain but the great weight of the war was borne by the U.S. In that war Russia was never an ally. Russia just did not enter that war. All during the war years Russia remained on friendly terms with Japan, maintained an embassy in Tokyo and a vast espionage system. Japan kept her embassy in Moscow. From December 7, 1941, the date of the attack on Pearl Harbor to August 9, 1945, Russia took no part in the war on Japan. On August 9, 1945, when Japan's defeat was already complete and surrender was only a matter of days, Russia declared war on Japan, marched into Manchuria and Northern China and other Japanese strongholds and into Northern Korea.

Japan surrendered five days later. Thus without striking a single effective blow and with only five days of nominal fighting, Russia, with the complete consent of the American government, took all the fruits of that war. She communized China, took over Manchuria, Outer Mongolia and Sinkiang, three provinces comprising one-third of China, as Russian satellite states. She dominates the rest of China, despite a smokescreen now and then of fierce hostility between the two, and she successfully managed with the guidance of the Insider Conspirators to engage the U.S. in both the Korean and Vietnam wars. Before entering the war Russia used every means in her power to give the war in the Pacific such a direction that she would achieve her aim without striking a blow. Her objectives were: (1) a victory for the Communist revolutionary armies in China; (2) the acquisition of the Kurile Islands, (3) of Sakhalin, (4) of Manchuria, Outer Mongolia and Sinkiang -- the northern part of China, (5) the conquest of Korea and (6) to share with the U.S. the occupation of Japan. She achieved all her ambitions except that of No. 6, sharing the occupation of Japan -- just think of it after only five days of nominal fighting.

Stalin admitted that two-thirds of all the war material plus much else that Russia had used in the war came from the U.S. Now all that being true, could any man in his (right) senses suppose that Americans would expend four years of frightful war to free the Pacific from the Japanese and then hand it over to the Russian Communists, that America would engage Japan's powerful forces throughout the Pacific challenging her navies all over that ocean and her armies in a hundred widely separated islands -- at the sacrifice of 200,000 American casualties, the loss of much of her navy and air force and the expenditure of billions of dollars, and then turn the fruits of all that fighting over to the ruthless tyranny of Russia. Yet, Stalin set out to accomplish precisely this, and succeeded, Stalin who depended on the U.S. for two-thirds of all his fighting material in the war in Europe, and who walked off with Asia in his pocket without having to fire a shot, with the name of being at war with Japan for just five days. How could such a thing happen?

In a way it was quite simple when the kind of power the Insiders have achieved in this century is understood. Any other answer just does not fit the situation. This is how it happened. The Japanese, like the Germans, were suing for peace for a full twelve months before it came. Not being at war with Russia they were using their embassy in Moscow to send out feelers. Stalin, bent on his own ambitions for Japan, naturally used such feelers to suit himself. The Japs next got in touch with General MacArthur himself and put certain proposals for peace. As it happened their proposals were exactly the conditions on which peace was finally brought to Japan. General MacArthur, the commander-in-chief of the American forces fighting the Japs, accepted the proposals, and took the necessary steps to bring the war to an end as speedily as possible. What happened next baffles belief, but it happened.

Two days before Roosevelt left for Yalta - and seven months before the final surrender of Japan - he, Roosevelt, received from General MacArthur a 40-

page memorandum. It contained an unofficial but authoritative offer of peace from the Japanese on precisely the terms on which the war in the Pacific was finally settled. MacArthur urged that negotiations be opened on the basis of these overtures. Now consider this: Roosevelt did not even take the memorandum to Yalta. It reposed on the files of the high command and became the basis of the final American demand for Japanese surrender seven months later - *after* the holocausts of Iwo Jima, Okinawa and the *atom bomb. So the atom bomb need never have been dropped.* The Japs knew the war was over in all but name, the Americans knew the war was over, rather the insiders, Roosevelt's bosses, knew it. Roosevelt dismissed the report from MacArthur with the remark, "MacArthur is our greatest general and our poorest politician."

The three top military and navy commanders in the Pacific and Leahy, the President's adviser, all opposed agreeing to let Stalin come into the Pacific war, but General Marshall, Head of the Joint Chiefs of Staff, sided with Roosevelt. It was said at the time by the odd person who suspected the existence of a higher conspiracy than that of Communism, that one of the mysteries of the war was the manner in which, at every turn, some influence could reach Marshall's mind to induce him to comply with the precise schemes being nurtured by Stalin, or more precisely by Stalin's secret and mysterious bosses. Where and when did the dangerous policy of allowing Stalin into the Pacific war just five days before it ended originate? Edward Stettinius says that the pressure for it began as early as 1943, and that Harry Hopkins, the mystery man, who was certainly Roosevelt's evil genius, appeared at Cairo bringing a memorandum urging that Russia be brought into the Pacific war. Every consideration of peace in the Pacific after the war that Russia be kept out of the war. Some consideration for the idea might have been reasonable in 1943. By 1944 it was preposterous. By 1945, when Roosevelt made the agreement, it was sheer madness, that is by ordinary standards of behaviour in either peace or war.

No explanation is possible except that Roosevelt acted as the tool of the top secret insider conspirators, who in all their dealings never lost sight of the idea of total world domination, and no better way of bringing that about than by foisting the Communist way of life on the unsuspecting peoples of the world, whether by outright war, or by such subtle intrigue that not a shot need by fired. In point of fact a book has been written on the take-over by the Communists of Czechoslavakia, called *And Not a Shot was Fired*.

But, strangest of all, this agreement was made at Yalta by Roosevelt in a secret meeting with Stalin. Even Secretary of State Stettinius, who was at Yalta, was not permitted to be present, and later, when he asked Roosevelt what had been done there, Roosevelt put him off. Only the Communist, Alger Hiss, was permitted to attend Roosevelt - Hiss, the secret Soviet espionage agent, and then high-ranking political adviser of the State Department and member of the Institute of Pacific Relations, a body funded by the Rockefeller and Carnegie Foundations, which for years had been preparing the American public by books and magazine articles to accept Chinese revolutionaries as not being in any way connected with Communism, but merely idealistic, well-intentioned agrarian reformers. The same line was later to be sold to the gullible American public on Cuba.

At Yalta Roosevelt agreed not only to let Stalin send his army into the Asiatic war but also to provide arms for a Russian army of 1,250,000 men, then on the Manchurian border, thus enabling them to march into China. Even James F. Byrnes, who was present at Yalta as Roosevelt's top adviser, and who later became Secretary of State was never told of these agreements, and President Truman did not know of them when he entered the White House as President on the death of Roosevelt. But Hiss, the Communist agent in the State Department, he knew.

Whittaker Chambers, in his book *Witness*, tells that the moment the Hitler-Stalin pact was signed in 1939, that led to the outbreak of the war in Europe, Roosevelt was told by his top security aid that Hiss was a Communist agent and the answer Roosevelt made him was "Go jump in the river." Hiss was later commissioned to write the Constitution of the United Nations, and become its first Secretary, but we must get back to the Yalta Agreement.

By its means Stalin was able to invade Manchuria, which Russia holds, the Kurile Islands and Sakhalin, which were conceded to him at Yalta by Roosevelt, and under this agreement he moved into Northern Korea. He was also able to make contact with the Chinese Communist armies in North China and begin to arm them adequately, for the most part with the arms surrendered by the Japanese to the Russians.

It was at this point -- after the war in the Pacific had ended as a result of American arms -- that the real operation got under way in Washington to bring about the defeat of Chiang Kai-shek and to deliver China and Korea to the Communists. The subtlety, the satanic cleverness and the sheer wickedness of what followed is so appalling that it is difficult to credit. Russia had her plans well laid. She was determined to bring about a successful revolution in China, to attach Manchuria, Outer Mongolia and Sinkiang to her own Red empire by making them into Russian satellite states, and to make all of Korea into a Communist state. This enterprise involved the liquidation of Chiang Kai-shek's government. And this Russia's agents launched with a clear-cut propaganda line. They set out to sell to American politicians, American newspapers and magazines and to every organization of information and opinion the following propositions about China:

> That Chiang Kai-shek represented the dying feudalism of old China and was an enemy of democracy;
> That his government was corrupt and would squander any aid received from the U.S.;
> That, on the other hand, the so-called Chinese Communists (a) were not really Communists but agrarian reformers and (b) were really democrats while Chiang was a fascist;

That the only hope for a permanent peace in
Asia lay in recognizing Stalin's legitimate
claims in Asia and in doing business with
him;
And, as the first stage in the liquidation of
Chiang Kai-shek, they demanded that he be
compelled to admit the Communists into his
government (with their army).

The malignant cleverness of this whole plan is
seen in that they did not demand that China be turned
over to the Reds -- merely that Chiang take them into
his government. Considering what a handful of secret
Communist agents in top positions in the American
state department were able to accomplish, what
would a whole horde do in China if they were taken
into the government, accompanied by a huge army,
armed and equipped, don't forget, with mostly
American war materials, plus what the Japs had surrendered.

This was the collection of ideas which the Institute
of Pacific Relations, funded, remember by the Rockefeller and such like Foundations, set out to sell to the
American people and to all members of the American
government not in the know, which of course meant
the vast majority. The Insiders do not personally like
to soil their hands with anything so raucous as
politics. Control is what they want, and that of all
parties.

This then was the way it was back in the war years,
when Russia was the "noble ally" and when even the
informed American knew very little about the art of
Red propaganda and still less about the political

structure of China. The American public, but above all its political leaders not belonging to the inside circle of the Insiders, was profoundly ignorant of Asia and of the shrewd techniques of Communist thought control. But there were specialists on Asian affairs, all trained in the Institute of Pacific Relations, now well versed in Communist methods, and they were all placed in the right places in the State Department and in the media, where they could do most harm.

Pro-Red books began to pour from the printing presses written by those trained in the Institute of Pacific Relations. Suddenly China and the little understood politics of Asia became of vital interest to the American people. Statesmen, journalists and editorial writers had to understand the background of that Asia in which so much was happening. And it was necessarily to these books that they turned. These books became a pool of poison which distorted all the available evidence on the struggle in Asia. In the *New York Times* and the *New York Herald Tribune*, as well as in other reputable review journals, these books were given glowing reviews. This is not hard to understand when one realizes that the *New York Times* for instance is well connected with Wall Street financial interests.

At the same time only seven books favorable to the regime of the Chinese government appeared, and every one of these was blasted in the reviews written by the same review journals all written by men and women from the Institute of Pacific Relations, now functioning as literary critics. Books would be written by these representatives of the Institute and their pals from the same Institute would review them in all the best places, giving glowing accounts of what they contained.

The following is a list of 14 books published in these critical years, and written by IPR members, as they are familiarly known:

Unfinished Revolution in China, by Israel Epstein.

United States and China, by John K. Fairbank.

Report from Red China, by Harrison Forman.

Journey from the East, by Mark Gayn.

New Frontiers in Asia, by Philip J. Jaffe.

Solution in Asia, by Owen Lattimore.

Making of Modern China, by Owen and Eleanor Lattimore.

Situation in Asia, by Owen Lattimore.

China's Wartime Politics, by Lawrence K. Rosinger.

China's Crisis, by Lawrence K. Rosinger.

Battle Hymn of China, by Agnes Smedley.

Challenge of Red China, by Guenther Stein.

Chinese Conquer China, by Anna Louise Strong.

The Phoenix and the Dwarfs, a play by George R. Taylor

It would be impossible for space reasons to outline the contents of these books, save to say that in varying degrees they promoted the whole line of those who favored the plans of Stalin in Asia, emphasizing that the so-called Chinese Communists were not really Communists and that Chiang Kai-shek's regime was the instrument of the corrupt and wealthy interests of old China. The most damning feature of these books was the manner in which the accounts changed as Russia's propaganda plans changed.

At one time Chiang was painted as a tool of the reactionaries. Then the propaganda altered, and began to advocate not the liquidation of Chiang, but a policy called "Unity in China", under which it was urged that Chiang should take the Chinese Reds, along with their army, into his government. Chiang was even praised, urging all Chinese to unite under the common enemy, knowing well that you cannot unite with Communists. As fast as these books appeared giving the Communist line for China -- mostly written by IPR members or associates -- they were given immediate and high acclaim in leading journals in reviews written by other IPR staff members. So it was a case of I stroke (scratch) your back and you stroke (scratch) mine. Millions of words poured from the printing presses praising the Communist line.

The gravity of this enterprise in mind control cannot be overestimated. At this time, editors, editorial writers, publicists, teachers and political commentators were rushing to the new books for the facts about this Asiatic world into which America had been suddenly plunged. The whole episode reveals the possibilities of propaganda and thought control of a high order. The organizers were expert and highly organized and had mastered the strategy of inserting their poison into some central and unsuspected pool of information.

The lies and half-truths in these books and in a few professional magazines began to color the news and opinions of the American press, and in the pulpits, classrooms and political organizations all over the country. And the central agency which carried on this extraordinary experiment in mass poisoning was the Institute of Pacific Relations, funded by the Rockefeller and other billionaire Foundations with headquarters in Wall Street. There was a bunch of other organizations especially devoted to the interests of Russia and the Russian Communists. One of these was the Russian War Relief, Inc. The International Workers Order was also a Communist front, and yet another was the American Russian Institute. There was another unit organized by the American League for Peace and Democracy -- a notorious Communist front -- called the China Aid Council. Mrs. Edward C. Carter was its chairman. Her husband, Dr. Carter, was a contributor to the magazine *Soviet Russia Today* and wrote in that journal a defense of the infamous Communist purge trials of the thirties.

When Roosevelt, a top agent of the Insider Conspirators, became President of the U.S. in 1933 one of his first actions was to recognize the Communist government in Russia. This saved it from economic collapse and in the U.S. itself gave carte blanche to all the writers and Communist front-men mentioned above to do what they liked. In 1947 Israel Epstein wrote a book called *Unfinished Revolution in China*. Epstein was a Communist. The book was published by Little, Browne and Co., whose editor at the time was a party member. It argued for precisely the kind of settlement as that by which China was eventually settled. Owen Lattimore, described as a conscious pro-Communist all his life, was asked by the *New York Times* to review the book.

Here the devious and crafty IPR really got down to work. It was a book written by a Communist, reviewed in the best places by a top pro-Communist and published by a well-known American publishing house with a Communist editor. The head of the IPR wrote the publishers to send copies to senators concerned with the issue. The *New York Herald Tribune*, the *Daily Worker* and the *New Masses* agreed heartily with Lattimore's review in the Times.

The result of all this propaganda whose sole object was to prepare the ordinary, ignorant-of-such-matters, unsuspecting American citizen who had contributed so much to a hard fought war that what was to come was best for China and the world. With the American public tired of war and its aftermath and now being told these people at the top in the State Department knew what was best to do in the situation, the public representatives, not wised up or in any way connected with the Insider conspiracy, went along with whatever was decided at the top, and the conspirators and their agents at the top knew exactly what they were doing.

China is a vast nation, and at the end of World War Two much of it was in the grip of age-old feudalism. Chiang Kai-shek was trying to lead this vast nation towards a measure of republican government. Mao Tse-tung led a Red revolutionary army which was a puppet of Stalin. No government is perfect, Chiang's was not, but it was infinitely to be preferred to that of Stalin's stooges. Furthermore Chiang's government was Chinese -- not a satellite of another state. Chiang was a man of high character and noble ambition. His purpose was to lead his country to a form of republicanism modelled on that of the U.S. It was in the interests of free men everywhere, and those desiring to be free, to aid Chiang. Yet this was not to be. American aid went to the Communists, not to Chiang. General Marshall was to boast at the time that with a stroke of the pen he disarmed Chiang. So startling and incredible as it may seem, it was with American arms that Chiang was driven off the mainland and onto Taiwan.

Chiang's government had been admitted to the UN as a full member and was still recognized as such. When Chiang set up in Taiwan the U.S. made a solemn agreement with Chiang that the U.S. would defend militarily its independence and that as many refugees as could be accommodated there would be helped to get to Taiwan. Taiwan is the same size as the 26 counties of Ireland. It has the second highest standard of living in the Far East, next to Japan.

Let the reader never lose sight of the main objective of the Insider Conspirators -- world domination. The UN was structured to be the nucleus of that world domination or world dictatorship. This being so, the Insiders couldn't afford to have tiny little Taiwan representing the Chinese people, so a way had to be found to get Taiwan out and Stalin's stooges into the UN. Little old Ireland was invited to join the assembly, that is the so-called free 26-county part of it. When one considers today the fate of Poland, Afghanistan, Cambodia, every Irishman should hang his head in shame that it was our ambassador to the UN who year after year brought up the question of just discussing whether Communist China should be admitted to that body. Year after year, the proposal would be turned down in the knowledge that one fine day when the time was ripe all would be accomplished, the Insiders would get their way.

We now come to the Nixon era in this jigsaw puzzle of fitting all the pieces into a Communist world ruled by the Insiders. Number one messenger boy for the Insiders was Mr. Henry Kissinger. He is sent to Communist China where the red carpet is laid out for him. During those same years, Mr. David Rockefeller as head of the Chase Manhattan Bank pays the Chinese Reds a visit. He too gets a red carpet welcome. Nods and winks are exchanged and before you know where you are Communist China is a member of the UN and Nationalist China is expelled, not that belonging to such a Tower of Babel is any honor. The sooner any self-respecting country gets out of it, the better for itself.

During the Carter years in the White House, ordinary Americans began to waken up to the awful truth that Jimmy Carter, who never told a lie, was working far harder for the spread of Communism than any top-ranking Communist, so they swept him clean out of office. But is the world any safer from the Communists under President Reagan? He has agreed to sell arms to the Communist Chinese. What does any Communist want with arms except to use them to communize the whole world. (Great Britain has agreed to sell Communist China Rolls Royce engines for their aircraft.) When Reagan was elected one commentator remarked that the cowboy had been driven into the corral and he never knew what had happened.

In selling military arms to China, America made no binding agreement that such arms must never be used against Taiwan with which America had a solemn agreement to protect the island with all military aid necessary. There is now grave danger that little Taiwan with its 17 million people (roughly half of them refugees -- can't you imagine their fate!) will be subverted, taken over and liquidated by totalitarian Red China. We are confirmed in this opinion by the following letter from the Bishops of Taiwan: "To Bishops of the world, to all Christians, to all men committed to justice." This is the letter:

"Brothers, we pray that Our Lord Jesus may grant you the peace that He has won for us through His sacrifice.

"Shepherds of our people: Although our Christians represent but a small minority of the population living in Taiwan, the Lord has commissioned us to shepherd the entire flock of the people of the land. The College of Bishops, under the active presidency of our Holy Father the Pope, have also established us as pastors in service to these people who are most dear to our Heavenly Father and who have been redeemed by the Blood of Jesus. It is as shepherds that we address this letter to you.

"Our islands shelter a population of seventeen million inhabitants, which is more than the population of Australia or of Holland, or of Switzerland; more than that of 120 among the 160 independent nations of the world. Seventeen million men, women and children who are born and who die, live and labor, experience joy and sorrow, who love and who pray and to whom our Lord Jesus 'has given the power to become sons of God'.

"Seventeen million inhabitants who, for the first time in the history of China, and after thirty years of unremitting work, have succeeded in raising substantially their standard of living and distributing equitably their hard-won prosperity. They have built a society which, although not perfect, gives them the possibility to live in freedom and in security from want. It provides them with opportunities to develop, to cultivate their talents and to serve God, each one according to his conscience. 'The Glory of God is man fully alive.'

"Seventeen million persons whose destiny is at stake. Our people, in fact, have recently been flung into the throes of uncertainty. They see the hard won fruits of their labor escape them, they become victims of international rivalries, while an indifferent and insensitive public opinion looks the other way. The political and diplomatic means of expression are gradually removed from them. The cultural, scientific, athletic sports and other assemblies of the international community are being closed to them. And they find themselves pulled into a mechanism of destruction, against their own will.

"Before it is too late, the voice of the shepherds must make known to the world the anguish and the distress of their people.

"The situation: It is common knowledge that thirty years ago, in 1949, the Peking regime assumed power

on the Chinese mainland. Being an island, the province of Taiwan was spared the fate of the other provinces of China. About two million refugees from the continent found safety here among eight million local inhabitants. Together, and with the aid of friendly countries, they developed this territory until it has now become a modern industrialized country whose population has almost doubled.

"While a great number of governments of the free world continued to give us diplomatic recognition, the geographic situation of our islands protected our freedom until, in 1954, the United States made it secure by a treaty of mutual defense.

"*In the course of time, one after another, the governments of the free world switched recognition to the Peking regime,* and in 1971, the United Nations decided to exclude us from their assemblies. Our population reacted with energetic courage to this gradual process of political, diplomatic and cultural isolation, confident that the community of nations could not deny them the possibility of survival in freedom. Our confidence was all the more natural, since we had always tried to contribute our share to the brotherhood of nations, as evidenced by the technical aid we provided during many years and are still providing to other developing countries, and by the humanitarian assistance that we are continuously rendering to the Vietnamese refugees, without any support from the United Nations.

"Finally and very recently, the United States, the guarantor of our liberty, decided to break diplomatic relations with our government and bring to an end the

141

solemn treaty of mutual defense. Like most of the other nations who recognize Peking, they declared that 'Taiwan is part of China'. By this ambiguous declaration the 'Taiwan question' becomes an 'internal matter' of China, while Peking is recognized as the only government in China; the legal title of Taiwan is handed over to Peking and our people are thrown aside, against their will, abandoned to the mercy of the totalitarian regime they abhor.

"This regime controls a population fifty times more numerous than our own, it occupies a territory three hundred times larger than Taiwan, and it disposes of enormous resources. Any economic or military advantage that may still be ours can but wither away under the weight of such a power. Fearing to offend Peking, the Free World is presently unwilling to guarantee our freedom by something more concrete than wordy declarations. What will it do when, eventually, this 'internal matter' is liquidated at the expense of our liberty?

"Quite naturally, this situation casts great anxiety upon us: our fate appears sealed entirely without our consent, and while everyone remains unconcerned, doubt is creeping into our hearts and could undermine our collective endeavor. Yet, we refuse to give up.

"*What is at stake for us*: Being of one heart with our population, we acknowledge but one China, one culture, one nation, one territory, but we repudiate with all our strength the regime that enslaves our brothers on the mainland. Facing the threat of the same fate which befell them, we affirm our determination to do all in our power to save our freedom and the freedom of our families. We ask you to try to understand what is really at stake for us.

"We seek no privilege, we ask for no favor, we are not recoiling from that suffering which is the common lot of man. But we absolutely cannot accept to be robbed of the inalienable right of every human being to live freely according to his conscience. The society we built with much toil is far from perfect, but it offers to each of us a chance to develop as fully as possible while respecting the rights of his neighbors. We want to protect that society for ourselves and for our children and, if some day it becomes possible, we wish to offer it as a model to our countrymen on the mainland.

"We are not shirking the sacrifices required by the service of our fellow men. We are not afraid of giving up our life style, our customs, our comforts, if the welfare of our brothers, especially that of the smallest among our brothers, requires it. Everyone knows that the Chinese people are capable of enduring great sufferings. Centuries of history, on both sides of the Taiwan Strait, attest to this fact. Poverty, *which we have so recently conquered*, does not frighten us, even if it is unjustly re-inflicted on us. We can endure material oppression, the direst deprivations, vexations and injustice itself. What we refuse to accept is to be denied the freedom to think what our intelligence and our conscience shows us to be the truth, the freedom to listen to the voice of God in our hearts and to live in conformity with His call.

"It is neither material well-being nor selfishness that impels us. It is simply the desire to live as human beings, to whom is offered the dignity of being sons of God, and to ensure that this same life will be the lot of our children.

"We refuse to become as human cattle. We refuse to have our thoughts dictated to us in defiance of the nobility bestowed on us by the Creator. We refuse to be turned against our will and our conscience, into puppets of a false ideology that we spurn. We know through the personal experience of many among us that this is the fate awaiting us if we weaken in our resolve, or if the world forsakes us.

"The press of the Western World is presently making itself the echo of a movement towards 'democratization' by the Peking regime. Our experience, closer to the actual facts, tells us that such movements appear regularly on the Chinese continent, and are forerunners of a stricter repression to follow. These movements are carried out according to the policies of Hegelian dialectics, and forever aim at tightening the hold of the regime upon the population. True liberation of the human person would be the negation of the regime, and a number of years would be necessary to ensure the credibility of such a radical change.

"*Fatal dialogue*: We do not expect our situation to change overnight. The process will last as long as necessary to avoid violent clashes with public opinion that would provoke unwanted reactions. But once started, the process will prove irreversible.

"As an initial step in the process, we are asked, innocently enough, to engage in dialogue. Chinese popular wisdom calls this 'pulling the tiger's whiskers'. A sad and already long experience shows that such a 'dialogue' leads inevitably to total and unconditional surrender.

"Can we honestly close our eyes to what happened after World War II in every single East European country? Can we honestly forget Vietnam where the most solemn agreements, guaranteed by great powers, were endlessly thwarted, leading to the final defeat of a people who refused to submit to the totalitarian ideology of a minority? Can we ignore that the inhabitants of that region, who heroically endured thirty years of a horrible and inhumane war, are unable to endure the oppression of that same ideology and, at overwhelming risks to their lives, flee their country by hundreds of thousands? So many tragic facts cannot be lightly ignored or unconcernedly forgotten.

"When a door or a window opens to a typhoon, the entire house is soon blown apart. Our national experience, six times repeated, abundantly proves that the dialogue, in which we are asked to engage once again, simply means that we deliver ourselves, with shackled hands and feet, to the unscrupulous interlocutor. Is the world ready to give asylum tomorrow to seventeen million refugees? Is it not simpler and more humane to prevent such a catastrophe?

"*Importance of world opinion*: In the next few months we expect a series of 'fraternal gestures' that may reach the point of 'asking our help' for the modernization of the motherland. The purpose of these gestures is to destroy us if we accept them and to turn public opinion against us if we do not.

"If we accept relations with the Peking regime, they will take advantage of it to weaken us by fomenting dissension among us. Every society contains seeds of 'contradictions' and to exploit and aggravate them to the point of conflicts and clashes is a very well-known tactic. Any relation with us will thus be used to discredit us in the eyes of the world and have us appear as losers, undeserving of outside support.

"If we reject relations, it will be 'proof' that we are not reasonable, that we refuse the outstretched hand of friendship and that the only possible solution is to use force to subdue us.

"How can public opinion, with so short a memory, understand such an extremely cunning and wicked game? On the one hand, we shall be condemned as unworthy of being defended because we disagree among ourselves. On the other hand, it will be said that we only reap what we have sowed, because we are so unbending.

"Both our past experience, and the process of destruction in which we are trapped, give us a clear vision of the situation. But many people see only the present moment while remaining blind to a process that stretches over months or years. To many, the danger will appear remote, yet we know that once in motion, the cogwheels will not stop until we are crushed. The tactic consists precisely in gradually building a wall around us, a wall that will effectively prevent our friends from helping us when the danger has become obvious.

"Already today, from another angle, insidious propaganda tries to turn public opinion against us and confuse our people by sowing distrust against our government, questioning the value of our collective endeavor and blowing out of proportion any weak point in our achievements. To build a society takes a long time and the result is always less than perfect; to criticize and destroy it is a very easy task.

"Attempts at infiltration and subversion will inevitably compel the government to harden and tighten up its security measures which are indispensable, but this will bring an immediate and hypocritical censure upon us. Many other tactics -- old and new -- will be used to discredit and destroy us.

"It is of vital importance to us that public opinion throughout the world be enlightened as to the truth of the situation as it is worked out in actuality. A constant alertness is required to expose the dangerous tactics that aim at catching us into the trap of death.

"*Our hope*: We have been ordained as shepherds to lead our people, all of our people, to the Father. It is part of our mission to protect the dignity of man who was created in the image and likeness of God. However, the Christians in Taiwan are but an insignificant minority and should this totalitarian regime, intolerant of any conviction except its own, succeed in its schemes, we would be reduced to utter powerlessness in no time. This would spell out the end of our mission. It is therefore imperative that we now speak up, in the hope of preventing the gloom of darkness from falling upon our land and our people.

"We address ourselves to all our brother Bishops. Successors of the Apostles, the Lord has entrusted you with a universal responsibility. Do not let a part of humankind, however small it may appear to you, be thrown into a condition of mental and spiritual slavery, unworthy of men created by God and redeemed by the Blood of Jesus Christ. Do not allow their souls to be torn away from them, and the light of conscience lit up within them by the Creator, be extinguished.

"We turn to all who believe in Christ, the only Savior of mankind. In the name of the Lord, do all in your power to help save our people from the degrading bondage that threatens them.

"In the name of man's brotherhood, we appeal likewise to all men who love truth and seek after justice. Our sages of the past taught us not to do unto others what we do not want others to do unto us. As none of you wish to be abandoned to hopeless servitude, do not either forsake your seventeen million brothers who are on the brink of that very fate.

"We earnestly request that each of you try to penetrate, and exert your influence in having others penetrate, the real significance of the situations and the events that are hitting us so hard, and that you also find effective ways to spare us this lot.

"We are in the hands of God, as well as in the hands of our brothers. May the Lord, Who commands us to love one another, bless you for your fraternal empathy and love.

"Our people are ready to defend their liberty and to face their destiny. Although no one should expose himself to temptation, yet as Christians, we are ready to share the Cross of Jesus if such is the will of God. But we refuse, and we ask you to help us to avert, the destruction of that which makes us rational persons. The Creator has placed in us a spark of freedom which makes us human beings. He wants us to protect it, to cultivate it, and never to let it be crushed or destroyed.

"Since we are the shepherds of our people, our vision reaches horizons that are farther still. Beyond the limited designs of man we discern the coming of the Kingdom, the universal sacrifice of the Lord Jesus, a sacrifice which vindicates our hopes. We envision a Father's love which transfigures our labors and our sorrows. Whatever the outcome of our efforts, whatever the fate men have in store for us, we know that nothing can ever prevent the Lord's victory over evil. We deeply hope to be able to walk through this desert with all of our people and to discover, in the far beyond, the loving face of our Father."

Taiwan, March 20, 1979

Matthew Kia, Archbishop of Taipei
Joseph Kuo, Archbishop of Salamina
Stanislaus Lokuang, Rector Magnificus of Fujen University
Peter Tou, Bishop of Hsinchu
William Kupfer, Bishop of Taichung
Joseph Ti-kang, Bishop of Chiyi
Paul Cheng, Bishop of Tainan
Joseph Cheng, Bishop of Kaohsiung
Joseph Wang, Auxiliary Bishop of Taipei
Thomas Pai, Apostolic Administrator of Penghu
John Tsao, Vicar Capitular of Hualien

The Bishops of Taiwan, PO Box 36603 Taipei, Taiwan"

The above letter is a cry from the heart from the noble Bishops of Taiwan. It is addressed to their brother Bishops, the princes of the Church and through them to all mankind not yet enslaved under the terrible yoke of Communism. This letter exemplifies Catholic churchmen at their best as champions and defenders of the inalienable rights of their people. They say: "Every society contains seeds of 'contradiction' and to exploit and aggravate them is a very well known tactic." Taiwan may have some such 'contradictions', but not even the worst enemies of Free China could deny that it exemplifies the kind of justice, peace and progress which churchmen of all denominations are forever proclaiming as imperative to 'development' in the Third World.

This being so, why the silence concerning the above letter, this cry from the heart. Has even one person who reads this ever heard the above letter read out in his church on Sunday morning? A copy of this letter can be obtained from: *Approaches*, 1 Waverley Place, Saltcoats, Scotland, on receipt of a s.a.e. or equivalent.* I would urge every reader who has any heart to send for a copy to be sent to his Bishop with a request that it be read out at every Mass on some Sunday, so that free men the world over may hear of it.

Note well that Taiwan is the same size as the 26-county Republic of Ireland, yet it feeds, clothes and gives shelter to seventeen million people, each

*Extra copies of the Bishops letter can be obtained by writing to the publisher of this book, if you send a stamped self-addressed envelope.

with an eternal destiny, and with a right from his Creator to have available to him all the means of salvation which the Catholic Church was founded to supply. When we remember the fate of Cardinal Mindszenty, is that not the fate awaiting all the above-named princes of the Church if the tyrants from the mainland ever take over Taiwan?

We have often heard: You can't bomb a million Protestants into the Irish Republic, but the same important people who could use their influence would stand idly by if and when 17 million Chinese on the island of Taiwan are bombed into the greatest tyranny the world has ever known.

Chapter 9

IS PEACE POSSIBLE?

> And His mercy is from generation unto
> generations to them that fear Him.
> He hath shewed might in His arm
> He hath scattered the proud in the conceit of
> their heart.
> He hath put down the mighty from their seat
> and hath exalted the humble
> He hath filled the hungry with good things;
> and the rich He hath sent empty away.
> from *The Magnificat* St. Luke Chapter 1 vs. 50-53

The peoples of the world both in the slave world held by the Communists and in the so-called free world of the West are all haunted by the fear of a Third World War. What ordinary people do not realize is that we *are* at war. An all-out war is being waged against us right now. This is total war, not just military war. Most people think of war only in terms of bombs and guns. Now for the first time in history we face an enemy that has mastered the concept of *total* war. The World War III that rages around us right now is a political war, an economic war, a psychological war and a military war -- though the military aspect is the least important of all, but above all, we are involved in a spiritual war against principalities and powers, a fight to the death.

The only way that military strategy plays a role in the Communist blueprint, is in the form of guerrilla tactics aimed at creating internal chaos and anarchy to create the kind of conditions conducive for the quick seizure of power-centres by a small group of organized and well trained revolutionaries. It is the kind of military strategy you'll find in the Communist manuals of Lenin, Mao Tse-tung and Che Guevara. But even this kind of limited military activity could never succeed without the simultaneous waging of non-military war. The Communist guerrilla bands could never succeed without other Communists operating secretly among people to create the appearance of popular support, operating within the communications media to generate propaganda, and operating inside the government itself to create the necessary corruption, bickering, and apparent inefficiency to prevent that government from moving strongly against the guerrilla groups.

In Cuba, for instance, when Batista fled the country, an army of over 45,000 soldiers surrendered without a fight to about 1,800 revolutionaries under Castro. Few people were aware then or now that the General who surrendered those forces was himself a member of the Communist Party of Cuba -- a perfect example of the non-military strategy of infiltration and treason producing an apparent military victory.

The favorite weapons of Communist conquest are not engines of mass destruction in the hands of uniformed soldiers. They are instead propaganda, the slanted view of history, the preaching of hatred to incite civil disorder, the tactics of internal subversion, treason, blackmail, the smear, political assassination -- all committed by soldiers who wear no uniform and who claim to be loyal citizens of the target country marked for takeover from within. This is how Communism has spread across the globe, not with invading armies or bombs.

The Atom Bomb is the most powerful weapon in the Communist arsenal. But its power rests in its psychological effect, not its military effect. The Communists have gained more by using the Bomb as a psychological weapon than they ever could have by using it as a military weapon. Under the constant threat of nuclear annihilation the West has accepted concessions, compromises and defeats one after another. This would have been unthinkable without the spectre of a giant mushroom cloud fixed deep in everyone's subconscious. The Bomb as a pyschological weapon is being dropped on us all every single day.

An important part of the Communist war being waged on us with no let-up is the Peace Movement orchestrated and tightly controlled by Moscow. People have short memories. How soon the atrocities perpetrated on the innocent people of Cambodia are forgotten. The Boat People are still with us but we are deaf to their cries. They endured all the horrors of a thirty year war and stood their ground, but preferred to die in the open sea than live under Communist rule. That is their problem. We are all right Jack. Out of hundreds of Communist horror stories that can be cited, we give just one to remind the reader of what he may expect if Russia ever succeeds in spreading her errors throughout the whole world.

On the morning of March 15, 1961, over 200 Europeans and 300 Africans were murdered in a Communist terrorist raid in Northern Angola. This account is taken from a pamphlet published by the Portuguese-American Committee on Foreign Affairs, 20 Pemberton Square, Boston, Mass.:

On that morning, a group of some 400 terrorists attacked the experimental farm at M'Bridge. A survivor, Manuel Lorrenco Alves, relates what happened:

"The assault began at six in the morning and all the houses on the farm whether they belonged to Europeans, Africans or mulattoes, were attacked simultaneously . . . The women were dragged out of their houses together with their children. In front of their mothers, the terrorists then proceeded to cut off the legs and arms of the children, and then started to play a grotesque game of football with the twitching bodies. The women and girls were led away, stripped, raped and cut up."

The above is an example of things that are happening this very day right across a large part of the globe. These incredible acts of brutality are the deliberate, premeditated works of men whose sole purpose is the destruction of human life and human values. The masters of deceit who finance, control and promote the Communist cause everywhere, live in their penthouses in the West without the puppets who do their dirty work for them ever having the slightest suspicion of the role they are playing. The puppet masters care no more for the brutal death of millions of people than they do for the death of a fly. Their war is total, their most helpless and defenseless victims the unborn children of both East and West.

The enemy has mastered the art of inducing a feeling of utter defeat and helplessness on the part of those who should be in the forefront in the battle for good against evil.

But at Fatima Our Lady gave the recipe for peace in the world, warning that unless people turned back to God in penance and prayer that a second world war would come, that Russia would spread her errors throughout the world. The object of this book is to explain the nature of those errors, what Communism is in practise, and how it has been practised in every country where it has got a foothold. This particular kind of slavery is awaiting the whole human race if the Insider Conspirators succeed in spreading the Communist yoke to the rest of the world.

Just as the Insider Conspirators used and financed Hitler to make sure the 1939-45 war took place, they used the organizing genius of Lenin to give Communism a foothold in Russia and to spread out from there until it would encompass the whole world. Lenin had a plan: it was first to take Eastern Europe, then the Far East, then to surround that last bastion of free enterprise, the United States, with a series of Communist states, and having corrupted the youth of the U.S. with pornography, drugs and anti-patriotic brainwashing, Lenin believed the U.S. would fall into the Communist lap like a rotten apple. To date everything has gone according to plan.

At the end of the 1939-45 war the U.S. was so strong that if the whole world joined together to make war on her she could have beaten it in a matter of weeks. How then, if the armaments of the world are being piled up in a war of ideologies, the free enterprise system against the Communist system, that the arch-enemy, the Communists, could be installed on the island of Cuba, a mere ninety miles from her shore. The American people had been fooled into joining in two world wars against the wishes of the overwhelming majority of them, and all the fruits of the Second World War in the Far East were deviously handed over to the greatest criminal in history, Stalin; the propaganda was so cunningly devised, the man in the street in the U.S. had no idea what it was all about. He was told again and again and again that Castro was no Communist, just a benevolent agrarian reformer. Now Cuba is a Russian powerhouse sending troops, guns, missiles of all kinds to Africa and South America, and because of a craftily engineered agreement at the time of the so-called missile crisis between President Kennedy and the USSR, the Insiders arranged that the U.S. was not to interfere.

Jimmy Carter arranged the sell-out of Nicaragua to the Communists. The late President Somoza had just time to tell how the master-plan was carried out before he was assassinated. His book is called *Somoza Speaks*, as told to an American reporter, Cox. Now El Salvador is in the melting pot. The extent to which subversion has infiltrated and become a power within the Catholic Church can be seen from the following account taken from the magazine *Approaches*, Saltcoats, Scotland:

On October 2, 1981, the U.S. Under-Secretary of State sent a letter to all U.S. bishops in order to provide a far better understanding of the basic facts than much of the current reporting allows.

With his letter he enclosed a translation of an AFP dispatch which appeared in the *Diario Las Americas* of Miami, reporting the Salvadorean Bishops' "stupefaction" concerning the French- Mexican communiqué which recognized the Salvadorean guerrillas as a legitimate political force, the AFP dispatch continued: "The members of the Episcopal Conference of El Salvador state they are witnesses to the fact that in El Salvador a small sector of the public is in sympathy with the Marti Liberation Front and the Democratic Revolutionary Front which have lost the support of the people and are currently devoting themselves to spreading terror among the population."

The Bishops went on to note how the guerrillas are destroying goods and services of the people in order to create conditions "which would make it possible to take power and impose a Marxist-Leninist dictatorship."

The *Diario* dispatch stated that the Salvadorean Bishops consider the French-Mexican document to be "an intervention" in the internal affairs of their country, and the episcopate foresees "the renewal of the prolonged war of attrition with the consequent death of additional Salvadoreans."

The need for truth:

Catholics know that only the Church, the custodian of the sacrifice and of truth, could have offered the people what had been torn from them by the worldwide anti-Catholic revolution: the spirit of toleration and social peace-making, under the sign of respect for the truth. Respect for the truth is, in fact, the only safe criterion for telling a friend from a wolf, and the true Church from the present mystification of the Church which, in the name of the poor, sends doctrine, liturgy and those same poor to be pulped.

The post-Conciliar Church:

To get a true idea of the "post-Conciliar" Church, we should listen to Archbishop Rivera y Damas who took Msgr. Romero's place, in an interview he gave to Giorgio Torchia *(Il Tempo,* November 15, 1981): "We must admit that some priests have made a choice which is strongly political. I mean that there are some who work outside the country as agents of the Front. There are only a few of them, but they exist. One of them speaks on 'Radio Venceremos', the official voice of the insurgents. That means that there are some priests who do not think with the Church."

The Salvadorean Trojan horse:

"We are faced," Torchia continues, "with the thorny problem of an institution, the "Soccorso Giuridico dell' Arcivescavada" (Juridical Aid Committee of the Archbishopric) which is at the centre of a furious controversy. Its offices are inside the archbishopric.

It flourished in the shadow of the late Msgr. Romero. Its original duty was to denounce any show of violence and, as far as possible, to give sufficient help to the victims. But in reality it is controlled by a group of persons who are clearly in league with the revolutionary front, and it has become an organ of propaganda in favor of the armed opposition. All the figures about repression (but not about terrorism which rages in Salvador) come from this organism. The figures are certainly one-sided. Some say they are falsified.

"According to Msgr. Rivera y Damas: 'The Soccorso Giuridico is quite equivocal. It was an institution set up by the Church before Romero. Then it became too mixed up in politics. The mind of the Soccorso is unilateral. I have always said that if it is an organization of the Church it should be more impartial and should denounce what the Left does as well. But that doesn't happen. I think that, behaving in that way, it can't be called objective, though many of its denunciations are true.'

"But," continues Torchia, "is it, or is it not, part of the archbishopric?

" 'Yes', says Msgr. Rivera y Damas, 'it belongs to the archbishopric. But it should keep within its juridical field and give legal help and not be an information office.'

"Msgr. Rivera y Damas doesn't show it, but he is deeply embarrassed, for the Soccorso Giuridico is a weapon of propaganda in the service of the guerrilla front, and the archbishopric allows it to function within itself and in the name of Church."

Strange testimony:

That is the strange testimony of a member of the Catholic hierarchy who admits that the revolution has invaded the confines of the Church by the action of other ecclesiastics, but who refuses to identify the evil and still less to think of getting rid of it. That is yet another proof that Communism is intrinsically evil; just living with it corrupts the memory and the will, and makes a man forget that one is either with Christ the Lord or against Him, with the lying enemy.

According to the *National Review*, December 11, 1981, when the U.S. Bishops met in Washington at their national conference at which they urged the U.S. government to cut off all aid to El Salvador urging a broad-based political solution which meant negotiations with guerrillas, the hierarchy in El Salvador was extremely perturbed. It accordingly sent two of its members to make its position known to the U.S. Catholic Bishops at their Washington meeting before they voted on the resolution. Lamentably but predictably the two emissaries, General Secretary Msgr. Freddy Delgado and Vice President Bishop Pedro Aparicio were frozen out, which led some Washington cynics to observe -- especially after the *Washington Post* detailed essentials of the matter in a stunning and totally unpredicted lead editorial -- that civil politics is like the frolic of novice nuns when compared to the hardball of ecclesiastical politics.

Bishop Aparicio and Monsignor Delgado were accorded no place on the conference agenda to convey the official views of their peers. All the more troubling since the Bishop's home town, San Vicente, is in the very thick of the fighting, allowing them to speak with special information and authority. Indeed, had it not been for offices of the Apostolic Delegate, it is reported, the two churchmen would have been denied even a private meeting with a ranking officer of the conference board.

This then is the position within the Catholic Church in many countries, the Church founded by Christ, having the fullness of truth, and commanded by Christ to go teach all nations the truth in its fullness. Christ promised He would be with His Church all days until the end of time so that victory in the end is assured, as Our Lady promised at Fatima.

Victory will only come after much prayer, penance, and hard work. To discover the truth about the manner in which the Insider Conspirators, unquestionably the richest men in the world, are furthering the Communist system while pretending to oppose it, is extremely difficult. But the evidence is all there and well documented by some of the world's foremost scholars.

Pius XI in his encyclical *Quadragesimo Anno* gives this account of the conspiracy: "In the first place, then, it is patent that in our days, not wealth alone is accumulated, but immense power and despotic economic domination are concentrated in the hands of a few, who for the most part are not the owners but only the trustees and directors of invested funds, which they administer at their own good pleasure.

"This domination is most powerfully exercised by those who, because they hold and control money, also govern credit and determine its allotment, for that reason supplying so to speak, the life blood of the entire economic body, and grasping in their hands, as it were, the very soul of production, so that no one can breathe against their will.

"This accumulation of power, the characteristic note of the modern economic order, is a natural result of limitless free competition which permits the survival of those who are strongest, and this often means those who fight most relentlessly, who pay least heed of the dictates of conscience.

"This concentration of power has, in its turn, led to a threefold struggle. First, there is the struggle for economic supremacy itself; then the fierce battle to control the state, so that the resources and authority may be abused in economic struggles; finally the clash between states themselves. The latter arises from two causes: because the nations apply their power and political influence to promote the economic advantages of their citizens; and because economic forces and economic domination are used to decide political controversies between nations."

At the Second Vatican Council, Father Pedro Arrupe, Head of the Society of Jesus, made the following remarks, according to a UPI message dated December 27, 1965: "This . . . godless society operates in an extremely efficient manner at least in its higher levels of leadership. It makes use of every possible means at its disposal, be they scientific, technical, social or economic. It follows a perfectly mapped out strategy. It holds almost complete sway in international organizations, in financial circles, in the field of mass communication; press, cinema, radio and television."

There was a strong plea from bishops from all over the world that the subject of Communism be discussed at the Vatican Council, but apparently the power of the secret societies within the Church was so strong no such discussion was allowed to take place, in spite of Reverend Father Arrupe's warning just quoted. What then can be done? Is it possible that you the reader can be the pebble that will loose the avalanche of good that will conquer evil in the guise of the Communist movement, that is imposing a slavery the kind of which the world has never before known?

Yes, it is possible that you, the reader of this account of the manner in which Russia is spreading her errors can be the pebble that will loose the avalanche of good that will conquer evil.

To begin, it is necessary to take the message of Fatima seriously and to try to carry out the wishes of Our Lady.*

Next it is vital that a study be made of the Pope's *Encyclical on Communism*. First buy it and read it several times. Then gather around you three or four of your friends, discussing with them what you have read. Then it would be necessary to meet once a week for a meeting lasting about an hour, during which about two pages of the encyclical would be studied in depth, one person in the chair asking questions which would be written out before the meeting and

*Publishers Note: See this further explained in Section II of this book starting on page 177 and in Section III, starting on page 215.

passed round. Each week a different person would take the chair. Having studied the encyclical on Communism the two encyclicals on the condition of the working class should follow, *Rerum Novarum* by Pope Leo XIII and *Quadragesimo Anno* by Pope Pius XI. From there on there is an endless number of encyclicals on all the social problems of the day including those which warn of the dangers of belonging to secret societies.

It should never be forgotten that we are fighting principalities and powers who use human agents. When Russia was about to take a big leap forward in spreading her errors by marching on Afghanistan, the mind of the whole world was taken off her action by the sleight of hand of getting some Communist students to take American diplomats hostage in Iran, knowing full well that at some stage they would be let free. In the meantime the poor people of Afghanistan were forgotten and in no time the Insiders had Iran and Iraq at war.

Russia is now the dominating force on the African continent. They have oil facilities at Mogadishu, docking facilities at Mombassa, a large naval base at Dar-es-Salaam. They have a large submarine base on the island of Pemba just off the coast of Zanzibar. Further down the coast, they have two bases at Mozambique -- Laurenco Marques -- and if you come right down to Angola, they have a base at Luanda. They have an interest in Madagascar, they have a lot of shipping at Mauritius and Mauritius now offers full naval facilities to the Soviet Union. They also have a whole lot of shipping tied up in the Seychelles Islands.

It is well to remember that Russia could never move one hundred yards outside her own territory without the permission and the financial backing of the Insiders. The amazing thing is that very few politicians or economists or even Church leaders have very much (if any) idea about what is going on all around them. In 1960 Harold Macmillan, the then Prime Minister of England made a lightning tour of several African countries after which he made his famous "Wind of Change" speech at Cape Town. He was informing the world that the black peoples of Africa were about to shake themselves free from the shackles of colonialism and emerge as free and fully independent nations. Mr. Macmillan did indeed seem to know a thing or two for soon one former colony after another was transformed into what was supposed to be a free and independent nation, each armed with all the trappings of parliamentary government, each with a set of rulers elected on the basis of the principle of one man one vote.

What Macmillan did not tell the world was that the power that transformed Africa was *an invading imperialism of money*, in other words economic colonialism in a new and more sophisticated form replaced the old type colonialism.

As a result of the wind of change Africa has become one of the world's disaster areas, with millions in constant danger of death from starvation, violence and disease, and tormented with one of the world's biggest refugee problems. Boundaries were set about which the blacks were never consulted, often enclosing several different black nations, each with its own language and cultural heritage, which have been split into two or more parts by the present boundaries.

When the blacks themselves tried to alter those boundaries they soon learned how really "free" they were. Katanga, a province the size of Western Europe tried to free itself from the rest of the Congo or Zaire. Nothing less than the armed force of the United Nations was used to bomb Katanga back into what the people of Katanga regarded as an unholy alliance. Then Biafra tried to free itself from the rest of Nigeria, but Britain and the Soviet Union joined hands to crush the people of Biafra.

Why should the Insider-Conspirators want to do this? They wanted the administrative machinery of the old colonialist system undisturbed but transferred to black regimes of a kind so artificial and precarious as to be easily controlled by themselves. In this way the natural resources of Africa and even its people have been far more easily exploited than if the old colonial powers were still there. What was liberated was not its people but its natural resources for gobbling up by the Insider-Conspirators. In the same way that Henry VIII and his henchmen looked at the monasteries, the Insider-Conspirators looked at Africa, its gold, diamonds and other wealth.

World Government being their ultimate objective and the United Nations being the nucleus of that would-be government, black puppets were set up to represent their people, each given a vote in the UN.

Mini-states like Rwanda and Burundi each has a vote and more mini-states around the world like Vaniatu (population 91,000) all help to vote the way the Insider-Conspirators want them to vote.

Cuba is sending thousands of troops and the guns and bombs supplied by Russia to Africa. The Insider-Conspirators could call a halt to this traffic in 24 hours, if they wanted to, but it all goes according to plan, their plan.

The turmoil in North Africa and in the Middle East generally -- like the brook -- goes on forever, in order to push up the price of oil and so compounding the rate of inflation in the developing countries. Milton Friedman, the arch-monetarist economist, admitted recently that if the Middle East could be stabilized, the price of oil could be cut by two-thirds. When there is massive unemployment as a result of this oil price inflation, the peoples of the developed countries are more easily "set up" for takeover.

Pointers

* The Shah of Iran gave an interview to David Frost before he died, in which he made two significant statements. He made a pointed reference to the Insiders, saying " 'They' wanted to put up the price of oil so they decided to take one country out of the supply and they picked on mine."

   He also said: "Just consider -- the military head of NATO arrived on my doorstep one day, and gave me the day and the hour on which I was to leave my country -- how would your Queen like to be given such an order."

* The putting up of the price of oil has been causing chaos in the developed countries, bringing about a flood of bankruptcies, with the consequent chain reaction of unemployment and despair.

* Joseph Kennedy is reputed to have said to his son John when the latter was a candidate for the U.S. Presidential election: "Do you realize what you are doing? This year they can make you President, and next year they would kill you if you dared stand in their way."

* Krushchev was sacked under rather mysterious circumstances. Who would dare sack the dictator of the USSR? It was noticed that immediately before he was recalled from his holiday home on the Black Sea that David Rockefeller spent his summer holidays in Moscow -- strange place for one's summer holidays.

  It should be noted that his bank, the Chase Manhattan, occupies No. 1, Kark Marx Avenue, in Moscow.

* Later David was to visit Peking in connection with his banking interests there, giving high praise to the achievements of Mao, in an article in the *New York Times*.

The key to the power of the Insiders is their control over the creation (making out of nothing) and circulation of money. Through this power, the Insiders have created all sorts of controlling mechanisms -- the World Bank, the Export-Import Bank, the Bank for International Settlements. Their power to create money means that the whole human race is in debt to them.

The whole of Africa, Latin America, South- East Asia, part of the Middle East, in economic terms today is called the Third World. The Third World without doubt is collapsing under a tremendous problem, and that problem is the load of debts that it is carrying. The debts now piled on the backs of the Third World are staggering. By the end of 1981 the terrible debts of the Third World were in the region of $451 billion, and they are trying to scrape up, in interest terms alone, $88 billion a year and they haven't got a chance because their exports don't even cover the interest. The mind boggles at the size of one billion, let alone 451 billions. Some idea of the power of the Insiders over the world's money can be glimpsed from the fact that in the first three years of the seventies, 1970, 1971, 1972, there was more money created (made out of nothing and ownership claimed by the creators) in those 36 months than in the whole previous recorded history of mankind. This in turn has led to the runaway inflation of the seventies and eighties, and the fact that millions of men, who want with all their hearts to work, stand idly by, having not the foggiest idea why.

Gorta, a group which tries to help people in the Third World has this to say: one acre of desert properly irrigated will keep a family for a year. Gorta aids 240 such families. It says: there is room for 20,000 such families. In other words if they had the money which the Insiders create and control all this could be done.

171

Daniel Webster once said, "There is nothing so powerful as truth -- and often nothing so strange."

The problem of producing the vital needs of people such as food, clothing, shelter, was conquered a very long time ago. Such easy production of the essentials of life should have given man the greatest possible amount of freedom to pursue the things for which he has a taste and to develop his spiritual life. But this was not to be. The principalities and powers working through their agents have made of life a nightmare for millions of people, a nightmare of debt which it is impossible to repay. For the first time in history, potential mothers are afraid to have children lest they be unable to pay just the interest on the house mortgage.

Time is running out. The Insiders want nothing less than to create a world system of financial control in private hands able to dominate the political system of each country and the economy of the world as a whole . . . the individual's freedom of choice will be controlled within very narrow alternatives by the fact that he will be numbered from birth and followed, as a number, through his educational training, his required military or other public service, his tax contributions, his health and medical requirements, and his final retirement and death benefits. The Insiders want control over all natural resources, business, banking and transportation by controlling the governments of the world. In order to accomplish this they have had no qualms about fomenting wars, depressions and hatred, and most cunning of all by furthering the spread of Communism by pretending to oppose it.

The truth that will set us free is a deep knowledge of the social teaching of the Church established by Christ*, and by taking the first step towards understanding how the token (money) by which goods are exchanged is created and controlled by this secret group of Insiders.

The choice is between liberty and slavery. As one wit put it: plenty of wool and no markets, plenty of poor and no blankets. The world does not have to be like this. The answer so far as you, dear reader, are concerned, is what you are going to do about what you have learned from what you have read in this book, and remember it is only an introduction to the greatest whodunit the world has ever known.

The people of the captive nations look to the so-called free West for salvation. How little they realize that their masters and ours are merely biding their time until we are all enclosed in the same net. Then we can expect that the tortures now endured by them will be even greater when no one is free anywhere to question what they do. Our one advantage is that we can expose their plan while there is still time.

"I will put enmity between thee and the Woman; between thy seed and Her seed. She shall crush thy head and you will lie in wait for Her heel" — *Genesis*. 3:15

*Publishers Note: See Section IV starting on page 221 of this book for a good introduction to this subject.

POSTSCRIPT

Since completing this book a news item in the *Irish Times* August 18, 1982, should strike terror into the hearts and minds of everyone who values the freedom to call his soul his own. According to the article, China maintains that Taiwan is its province and has argued that continued U.S. arms sales to the island was an interference in the affairs of the People's Republic of China, with which the U.S. established diplomatic relations on January 1, 1979. In a joint communique issued in Washington and Peking on August 17, 1982, the U.S. said that it did not seek to carry out a long term policy on arms sales to Taiwan. The U.S. said that its arms sales to Taiwan will not exceed, either in qualitative or in quantitative terms, the level of those supplied since 1979.

The U.S. also said it intended to "reduce gradually its sales of arms to Taiwan, leading over a period of time to a final resolution." China affirmed that its "fundamental policy" is to strive for a peaceful solution to the Taiwan reunification question.

The news item ended by saying that the UN Secretary-General, Mr. J.P. de Cuellar, arrives in Peking on the morrow on a four day official visit.

Yesterday it was the turn of the brave people of Hungary, Czechoslovakia, Poland and Cuba, who watched in amazement and stupefaction the richest and mightiest nations the world has ever known stand idly by while they were sold into slavery. Tomorrow it will be the brave people of Taiwan unless the men of goodwill everywhere come to their aid.

Section II

Our Lady's
Urgent Appeal
to Us in the 1990's

by
The Fatima Crusader

This Section is available in booklet form under the title *Our Lady's Urgent Appeal to Us in the 1990's*. (This booklet also includes a Rosary Novena booklet).

It is available from: **The Fatima Crusader**

In **U.S.A.:** P.O. Box 93
Constable, NY 12926

In **Canada:** 452 Kraft Road
Fort Erie, Ontario L2A 4M7

In **Philippines:** P.O. Box 1395
Metro, Manila 1099 - Philippines

In **India:** 6 R.R. Flats, Anthu Street
Santhome, Madras 600 004 - South India

It is hoped that many readers will obtain as many copies as possible and distribute them.

Already over 700,000 copies are in circulation.

Introduction to Section II

This section is an explanation of the Fatima Message. The Blessed Virgin Mary, our Spiritual Mother and the Spiritual Queen of all countries, urges all people, who are in danger of nuclear war and enslavement, to save themselves and their country by praying the Rosary and heeding Our Lady's full Fatima Message.

This section picks up where the author of *Fatima and the Great Conspiracy* leaves off. Namely - The Final Triumph over satan is given to Our Lady - "I will put enmity between thee and the Woman; between thy seed and Her seed. She shall crush thy head and you will lie in wait for Her heel." (Genesis 3:15)

It is at Fatima that the Triumph of Our Lady is promised and predicted in our lives. But it will not come without a struggle and Our Lady will not do it all alone. You must do your part. All this is explained to you more fully in this Section.

This section was first printed in *The Fatima Crusader* in 1982 and subsequently published in Booklet form, with the **Imprimatur** of the Bishop of Prince Albert, **Laurent Morin**, August 12, 1982.

This section has more than 750,000 copies in circulation. Extra copies are available from the publisher of this book.

PART I — WE MUST CHOOSE NOW

• God's Special Love for Us in the 20th Century

As you know, God in His great love for us, His people, whom He created in the 20th Century, gave us a most extraordinary favor, a grace reserved for our age, by sending His Most Holy Mother Mary to us at Fatima to promise us peace.

She came to three shepherd children to give us this message from God, a message of Hope and the promise that, under the leadership of the Blessed Virgin Mary and through Her intercession, the forces of Good would win against the forces of evil, and that this Victory for God on our behalf over the devil and his followers would take place in our time. We, indeed, then are most fortunate to be living at this time. Furthermore, we too can participate in this Victory. In fact it will be given as soon as enough of us rally to Our Lady of Fatima's Peace Crusade.

We know that we cannot demand of God to work a miracle in order to prove that a message comes from Him. St. John the Baptist, who was certainly sent by God to prepare the way for Jesus' public life, never worked a miracle. We also know from our Catholic Faith that God does sometimes work miracles and that real miracles worked in favor of God's message are certain proofs that in fact that message comes from God. Thus we can prove the teaching and works of Jesus in fact come from God.[1]

The message of Fatima is very rich in teaching content and certainly offers us great hope and very wise counsel for our troubled century. The story of Fatima and its message are very simple yet very profound. It is certainly a prophetic message for our times; one that we cannot ignore except at our own peril; and one confirmed by a great series of miracles at Fatima.

At Fatima, God, through the intercession of Our Lady, deigned to confirm this EXTREMELY IMPORTANT MESSAGE for the 20th Century by a most stupendous miracle, witnessed by over 70,000 people. Recent studies of the photographs show that over 100,000 people saw the Miracle of the Sun at Fatima, a beautiful and moving experience that was apocalyptic in its dimensions. "And there shall be signs in the sun and in the moon, and in the stars." (Lk. 21:25) Many people were cured on the day of the miracle and many conversions took place. The event of Fatima is still going on. "It will go on until Our Lady's final victory throughout the world."

• **We Must Respond Now**

Of course final victory is absolutely assured by Our Lady of Fatima as She said, "In the end My Immaculate Heart will triumph and a period of peace will be given to mankind." However, She tells us honestly and openly that the hour that the victory will come depends on us. Jesus and Mary want, much more than we do, that this true peace will soon come to the world and that all men will live in Peace and Harmony and Justice and Charity all over the earth, as God intended it to be when He created us. However, the Peace of God can only come when enough of us do what Our Lady of Fatima asks. There is no other route to true peace except by following Our Lady of Fatima's Peace Plan. Moreover, if we ignore God's Heavenly Mother and Her Message of Love and Her promise of help at this crisis in Human

182

History, then God, at Fatima, warns us that although peace will finally come to the world IT WILL BE AFTER MANY NATIONS ARE COMPLETELY WIPED OFF THE FACE OF THE EARTH AND THAT AFTER MANY GOOD PEOPLE ARE MARTYRED AND THAT THE POPE SUFFERS MUCH.

Footnotes to Part I

1. "Nevertheless, in order that the submission of our faith might be consonant with reason (see Rom. 12:1) God has willed that external proofs of His revelation, namely divine acts and especially miracles and prophecies, should be added to the internal aids given by the Holy Spirit. Since these proofs so excellently display God's omnipotence and limitless knowledge, they constitute the surest signs of divine revelation, signs that are suitable to everyone's understanding (see cans. 3-4). Therefore, not only Moses and the prophets but also and pre-eminently Christ our Lord performed many evident miracles and made clear-cut prophecies." (Vatican Council One, Denzinger 1790.)

Canon 3: "If anyone says that it is impossible for external signs to render divine revelation credible and that, therefore, men ought to be impelled towards faith only by each one's internal experience or private inspiration: let him be anathema." (Denzinger, 1812.)

Canon 4: "If anyone says that all miracles are impossible and, hence, that all accounts of them, even though contained in Sacred Scripture, should be classed with fables and myths; or that miracles can never be recognized with certainty and that divine origin of the Christian religion cannot be successfully proved by them: let him be anathema." (Vatican Council One, Denzinger 1813.)

Taken from Chapter 3 - Dogmatic Constitution onthe Catholic Faith, Vatican Council One, 24 April 1870.

PART II — OUTLINE OF THE CRISIS
(The Rebellion Against God)

- ## Introductory Look at the Contemporary Scene

Canadians and Americans are increasingly aware that America, in common with the rest of the world, is in a condition of crisis which seems beyond the capacity of human aid to alleviate. Evidence of stress and moral breakdown is all around us: there is crisis in family life as seen in the rising number of abortions, (over 23,000,000 in the U.S.A. alone from 1973 until 1989) and marriage breakdowns; the increase in drug abuse; the corruption of young and old by violence and sex (including perversions) shown more and more openly on TV and in the movies; immodest fashions; the lack of moral and religious education of our youth; threats of nuclear war; high and usurious interest rates which make it increasingly impossible for people to own or continue to own their own homes; the type of advertising which encourages people to go into debt to buy goods they do not need, furthering inflation and raising interest rates.

Within the Catholic community there are the additional concerns, for example: falling attendance at Mass, the decrease in the practice of Confession; the blatant undermining of the authority of the Pope and the Bishops; a growing awareness that, even in many Catholic schools, religious education is woefully inadequate; and fewer vocations to the religious life.

Certainly some of these problems can be (and are being) solved within the family circle, and by many men and women within their own spheres of influence. Nevertheless, many remain beyond the scope of the ordinary citizen. Governments, far from having solutions, have all too often created the problems by their legislation. Such a problem is abortion.

Chapter One

Remember Our Rights
Come Directly From God

Our rights to life, liberty, the right to private property, our right to freedom of conscience and the practice of the one true religion founded by Jesus Christ, are given to each human person directly by the Creator. No human authority has the authority from God to take these rights away. The state, too, may not even pretend to have such authority to deny us these fundamental rights, as all authority comes from God.

These rights come from God because God made us to live according to His Will and to accomplish our individual vocation. To fulfill our duty to God and our fellow man, since we are free and rational creatures with a material body, He has to give us the means and the necessary rights (authority) in order to achieve His Will.

Thus these rights are given directly to us by God. They are not given to us through the State but immediately and directly. The state's, the Government's, all the public authorities' purpose is to promote harmoniously the God-given rights of its citizens so that the citizens, in exercising their rights unhampered, may the more easily save their souls and glorify God. The state may not on any pretext (even a majority vote) take away our God-given rights EVER.

• Right to Life Under Attack

In the U.S.A. the Supreme Court has killed over
23,000,000 American citizens by ruling on January
22, 1973, that abortion is legal. These 23 million
violent deaths are many times more than all American
lives lost in all its wars. Similarly in Canada the
government and the courts, the public authorities and
their collaborators, have taken away the most fundamental right, the right to life, of over one-half
million Canadians; that is, over 500,000 human lives
have been murdered in this land — "the true north
strong and free" — in the past ten years alone. These
very violent and painful deaths in Canada due to
abortion in the past ten years are five (5) times more
than all the violent deaths that Canada has suffered at
the hands of her enemies, in all the overseas wars
(Boer War, World War I, World War II, and the
Korean War) in which Canada has fought since
beginning as a nation in 1867.[2]

• Rights of Jesus Christ our King Under Attack

The blatant, grave injustice of abortion committed
against the most innocent and the most defenceless
of our brothers also indicates something else. It shows
that many leaders in our countries — for example,
Members of Congress and Members of Parliament as
well as people in the courts and in many hospitals —
are in effect and in practice, declaring themselves
independent of Jesus Christ and His reign over our
countries and all their individuals and institutions.
The Bible tells us that Jesus is King of kings and Lord
of lords (Apoc. 19:16). As our King, He demands that
our legislators, laws, courts, and hospitals reflect His

law and that they do not contradict it.

Jesus Christ our King demands that all of us, particularly in our laws, really and effectively protect the lives of our unborn. In the words of the Vicar of Jesus Christ, Pope Pius XI, we are shown this grave obligation which is binding on legislators of all times:

"Those who hold the reins of government should not forget that it is the duty of public authority by appropriate laws and sanctions to defend the lives of the innocent, and all this the more so since those whose lives are endangered and assailed cannot defend themselves. Among whom we must mention in the first place are infants hidden in the mother's womb. And if the public magistrates not only do not defend them, but by their laws and ordinances betray them to death at the hands of doctors and of others, let them remember that God is the Judge and Avenger of innocent blood which cries from earth to Heaven." (Encyclical on Christian Marriage.)

This sin of abortion is the responsibility not only of legislators, but also of educators, and those who form the consciences of our people. In former times, it was the clergy who fulfilled their God-given role of properly forming the consciences of the people, but today it seems that many people take their guidance from the mass media, TV, movies and newspapers. Yet where are the newspapers and mass media to sound the alarm to warn us of this silent war waged against our own citizens?[3]

Therefore, since the laws of our country have been changed to protect the guilty (that is, those who commit abortion), and leave defenceless the most innocent, and since abortions are paid for with tax money, and since this injustice has not been vigorously opposed by the majority of Canadians and Americans, many of us, it would seem, are guilty in varying degrees before God for this "unspeakable crime" (Vatican II, Gaudium et Spes. Para. 51), which the Scriptures tell us "cries to Heaven for vengeance".

• The Attack by High Interest Rates

A third point of evidence of the crisis in America and elsewhere is the high interest rates, which cause great hardship to those many individuals who have to pay these rates on their mortgages and personal loans, and which are in themselves sinful. Such interest rates are an example of usury which is against the law of God and attacks our God-given right to private property. Great harm is done to the social fabric of our country by these interest rates because they decrease the number of real private property owners and they thereby further concentrate in the hands of the few, a greater economic power. As a result, over time, more and more people will be reduced in their real freedoms, for without true economic freedom, there will be very little real political or personal freedom.

The direct ownership of private property by very many people is one of the necessary pillars of personal and real political freedom for all citizens. On the other hand, when relatively few persons own or control the means of production, these few are able to impose their rule over the rest of society through economic pressure on individual wage earners, through manipulation of politicians and leaders of society, and through the control of the mass media by means of the power that their excessive wealth gives them.

• The Threat of Nuclear War

Another sign of crisis in America is the threat of nuclear war, which not only affects Canada but all nations of the world. This threat is real and beyond our human control. No matter how many marches we walk in, or letters we write to the editor, or lobbying done with the government, whether our country be aligned or non-aligned, there are declared enemies of our people and of course our way of life, who would use such weapons against us if they could do so with no tremendous inconvenience to themselves, unless we would voluntarily make ourselves their slaves. We do not have human power enough to resist them. Unless God does help us in this crisis, no human allies, not even the U.S.A. (as Sister Lucia has explained[4]) can save any free nation.

Chapter Two

Our God-Given Rights Openly Attacked

It is not only in the Right to Life, but also in other very important rights, that the Governments (federal and local) of Canada and the U.S.A. are gradually taking away — or are prepared to take away — our God-given rights. In Canada, for example: in the recent "Charter of Rights", the federal and provincial governments have written into the Charter the power for them to override any person's or any group's right to the free exercise of his/their conscience or religion. Some might say that we need not worry because no government will ever invoke this power to override individual consciences. If they never will do this, why did the governments write it into the Charter?

If governments will not accept in practice and in

law the idea that governments themselves are responsible to God and have authority to rule only from God
(and only so far as God authorizes them), then they,
in turn, will assume in practice that there is no other
greater authority than government. If this trend is not
reversed, they will, over time, demand absolute and
total obedience, even when their will is against the
Law of God and against the God-given and inalienable rights of its citizens.

- **The Struggle Between the Forces of Good and
  the Forces of Evil in Our Times**

We see, then, that modern governments in North
America and elsewhere have increasingly rejected the
concept of having their powers restricted by any
moral restraints, which means that they operate in a
moral vacuum and become increasingly totalitarian.

At this time, then, we must especially remember
the warning given by the great statesman, William
Penn: "If men are not governed by the Laws of God,
they will be ruled by tyrants."

And here are some statements of the Popes concerning our times: "There is room to fear that we are
experiencing the foretaste and beginnings of the evils
which are to come at the end of time, and that the Son
of Perdition, of whom the Apostle speaks, has already
arrived upon the earth." (From Pope St. Pius X Encyclical Suprema Apostolatus, 1903 — in reference
to the anti-Christian movement of Freemasonry attacking the Church from outside and the Movement
of Modernism subverting the Church from within.)

"The smoke of satan is seeping into the Church.
The tail of the devil is functioning in the disintegra-
tion of the Catholic World." (Pope Paul VI.)

• Deliberate Plans of the Forces of Evil

Let us not be deceived into thinking that these corrupting influences have come to our country and into the world and the Church without a deliberate plan of the enemies of God and the enemies of our country. Led by satan, these men have a deliberate plan to corrupt us, to deceive us, and to enslave us. Here is a quotation from one of the secret societies which plotted the overthrow of the Church and legitimate civil government. This Masonic society said that a dagger is not enough to bring down the Papacy, for another Pope would be elected, and that in order to bring down the Papacy,they said, "Let us not make Christians sin, rather let us corrupt Christian hearts." To quote them directly, they said:

"Let us spread vice broadcast among the multitude. Let them breathe it through their five senses, let them drink it in and become saturated with it . . . Make men's hearts corrupt and vicious and you will have no more Catholics. Draw away priests from their work, from the altar and from the practice of virtue . . The best poniard with which to wound the Church mortally is corruption." (Quoted by Father Denis Fahey, C.C.Sp., in his book, *"The Kingship of Christ and Organized Naturalism"* — pp. 18-19.)

Our Lady of Fatima warned that Militant Atheists would "**spread** their errors throughout the world" — if we did not heed Her warning. She also said that "certain fashions **would be introduced** which would offend Her Son very much." Our Lady indicated that our enemies had a deliberate plan to corrupt our faith and our morals.

192

• What is a Militant Atheist?

Militant Atheists are, by definition, people who not only do not believe in God, but who work and fight and use whatever means they can (they are not restrained by any considerations of right and wrong) to impose on the people their atheism. There is documented evidence of co-operation between the various branches of Militant Atheism to bring about their tyrannic rule over the whole world.[5]

Since the Militant Atheists cannot all operate openly because the people would wake up to the danger, many Militant Atheists in the Western World do not openly profess their atheism or their aims to deceive, to subvert, and to subject society under the oppressive yoke of Militant Atheism. The Militant Atheist is an extremely dangerous enemy. He is particularly dangerous to our Eternal Salvation because he will use force, if possible, and will use trickery as well, to try to impose his atheism on each one of us. To accept, for whatever reason, his doctrine is to deprive ourselves of Eternal Salvation, for it is necessary "for a man to believe that God exists and rewards those who seek Him" in order to be saved. (Hebrews, 11:6)

• Militant Atheists' Trickery

Let us not be deceived by the trickery of the Militant Atheists. Pray the Rosary daily in order to avoid their deceptions and lies. Let us also recall that many Popes over the past 250 years have condemned the sect of the Freemasons and its practices and its doctrines. Pope John Paul II, through the Congregation for the Doctrine of Faith, has recently reaffirmed the excommunication passed on any Catholic who joins the Freemasons. (See decree of February 17, 1981.) (See Nov 26, 1983 Declaration By Cardinal Ratzinger and the Holy Office.)

Besides the open Militant Atheism of the Communists who are spreading the lies of the devil by military might and by the subversion of our society, other diabolical errors and movements are afoot in our country and in the Western World such as Secular Humanism and also the planned decline of moral standards among the people, as evidenced by the widespread use of contraceptives and sterilizations, as well as increasing drug and alcohol abuse.

These errors against faith and morals are spread amongst our people by the devil and his henchmen on earth, and their spread forebodes badly for our country. Militant Atheists know that before they can conquer and enslave a country, they must first bring about the moral downfall of the people and enslave them to sin. Then they know that the people will not have the spiritual strength necessary to resist them and their plots, and their open military might, whereby they shall enslave the country — in a very evil, cruel and extremely painful slavery.

The Prophet Balaam in the Old Testament was asked to help defeat those who were then the People of God. Balaam replied to the enemies that they could not win because God is protecting His people. But Balaam went on to say to God's enemies that if they could get the People of God to sin enough, then God would not protect His people and then the enemies of God could win. So the enemies of God, then and now, follow the same battle plan: first get the people of God to sin enough — then the enemies of God will be able to win in war because God will have withdrawn His protection. Thus the Militant Atheists seek above all to corrupt Catholics — the People of God of the New and Eternal Testament — and they are succeeding to a great extent.

Footnotes to Part II

2. Vital statistics for abortions from Statistics Canada. Warfare statistics from the World Almanac.

3. Catholic Bishops meeting at Vatican Council II in 1965 were given a report which said that most of the mass media, including newspapers and TV, around the world, are controlled by a very small group of men who are militant atheists.

4. See Part IV of this Section II.

5. See, for example, Father Denis Fahey's book, *The Rulers of Russia,* where he shows that very powerful Militant Atheists in North America financed the Revolution in Russia in 1917. See Leon de Poncis' book, *Freemasonry and the Vatican,* which refers to the collaboration of 1943-1945 between Militant Atheists of East and West to divide the world between them, which collaboration resulted in the Treaty of Yalta, whereby Stalin and Soviet Russia were de facto given half the world.

See also the book, *The Antichrist,* published in 1981 and written by the late Father Vincent P. Miceli, S.J., Ph.D., an American priest who has taught at Pontifical Universities in Rome.The book is already in its 5th edition, and has an imprimatur from the Archdiocese of New York. In his book, Father Miceli gives the historical evidence and the theological background on the forces of evil, including recent examples of the inroads of the devil and his followers into North American society, international politics, and even into the Church Herself.

Part III — CAUSE FOR HOPE — OUR LADY

Let us lift up our heads and raise our hope in God, for He said that the Blessed Virgin would defeat the devil and his followers and his plots: "I will put enmities between thee and the Woman, and thy seed and Her seed: She shall crush thy head, and thou shalt lie in wait for Her heel." (Gen. 3:15.)

And the Blessed Virgin has come in our time at Fatima and promised us Victory in our time, over all these forces of evil. "In the end My Immaculate Heart will triumph, the Holy Father will consecrate Russia to Me. Russia will be converted and a period of peace will be given to mankind."

- ## Our Lady Forewarned Us About Our Present Crisis

Our Lady of Fatima prophesied and predicted that Militant Atheists would spread their errors throughout the world, and thus also throughout America if we would not listen to Her maternal warnings and simple requests. The errors of the Militant Atheists include those doctrines which teach us to ignore God, which teach us that our public laws and institutions need not conform to the Law of God, which teach individuals and families that the goal of human life is money, illicit pleasure and honor from worldly people, rather than teaching us that the most important purpose in each one of our lives is to save our souls and gain the eternal happiness of Heaven. The crisis in America and the world can still be overcome now, if we turn to Our Lady and do what She asks of each one of us at Fatima. In Her own words, She said, "If My requests are heeded, Russia will be converted and a period of peace will be given to mankind."

• The Fatima Peace Plan Is Our Only Hope

Each time Our Lady appeared to the three children at Fatima, She asked us to pray the Rosary. Our Lady also asked us to wear the Scapular.[6] In the final vision, on October 13, 1917, Our Lady silently held out the Scapular. Lucia has said the Blessed Mother wants everyone to wear it. "The Scapular and the Rosary are inseparable." Our Lady also said, "If people do what I tell you, many souls will be saved and there will be peace."

She told us there is no other solution whereby we are to achieve true peace and real social harmony and order than by following the Peace Plan and the requests She addressed through Her message at Fatima to each one of us. These requests have been summarized by Sister Lucia in the Peace Pledge Formula, which is as follows:

Dear Queen and Mother, who promised at Fatima to convert Russia and bring peace to all mankind, in reparation to Your Immaculate Heart for my sins and the sins of the whole world, I solemnly promise: (1) to offer up every day the sacrifices demanded by my daily duty; (2) to say part of the Rosary (five decades) daily while meditating on the Mysteries; (3) to wear the Scapular of Mount Carmel as a profession of this promise and as an act of consecration to You. I shall renew this promise often, especially in moments of temptation.

Padre Pio, the famous stigmatic priest, has said that when enough of us make and keep this promise to Our Lady, then Russia will be converted and there will be real peace.

• Sin is Destroying Our World Today

It is sin that is destroying the world today. Our Lady of Fatima said, "War is punishment for sin." Since not enough people are willing to grant the requests of Our Lady of Fatima and give up sin, what does the future hold in store for us?

A few months after the close of World War II — the bloodiest war in all history — Pope Pius XII warned: "Men must prepare themselves for suffering such as mankind has never seen."

The vicar of Christ indicated that we must prepare for suffering even worse than the deluge, which wiped out the whole human race except for Noah and his family; for suffering worse than all the wars and disasters that have been the long history of mankind.

Yes, this is what the future holds for America and the world — suffering such as mankind has never seen, unless a sufficient number of people still can be found willing to grant the requests of Our Lady of Fatima.

• Is There Any Hope left in the 1990s?

No matter how late the hour, so long as these threatened disasters have not yet struck, there is still hope of averting them if enough people will amend their lives and do what God asks. We read in the Old Testament (Jonas, 3rd Chapter) that Almighty God sent Jonas the prophet to warn the people of Nineveh that in 40 days their city would be destroyed. Upon receiving the news, the king immediately proclaimed fasting and abstinence, told the people to don sackcloth and ashes, to do great penance and give up the evil and iniquity in their hearts — and they did. Almighty God was pleased, and at the end of 40 days Nineveh was still standing. God had spared the city because enough reparation had been made.

We also read in the Old Testament (Genesis, 18th Chapter) that God would have spared the wicked cities of Sodom and Gomorrah had there been found ten just people in them.

Today, Almighty God will spare America, and even the whole world, from the horrible punishment predicted for us if, proportionately, the ten "just" can be found willing to make reparation — willing to follow the "peace plan from Heaven".

• **Victories of the Rosary**

Our Lady pleaded and insisted that people say the daily Rosary. Reparation holds back the hand of God from striking the world in just punishment for its many crimes. The Rosary is like a sword or weapon the Mother of God can use to cut down heresy and the forces of evil. It is most powerful, and many times has saved the world from bad situations like the one facing us today.

• **Lepanto 1571**

A few centuries ago, the Turks were over-running all Europe and seemed on the verge of wiping out Christianity. When all seemed lost, Pope St. Pius V organized a Rosary Crusade. He asked Catholics everywhere to pray the Rosary to ask Our Lady to deliver them from imminent disaster. When the day of the great battle arrived, the Christian soldiers literally went into battle with swords in one hand and Rosaries in the other. Thus on October 7th, the Feast of the Most Holy Rosary, one of the greatest military upsets in all history, took place at Lepanto. The little Christian fleet, very greatly outnumbered, defeated the mighty Turkish Armada and Christianity was saved — all through the power of the Rosary.

• Hiroshima 1945

The Rectory of the Assumption of Our Lady Church in Hiroshima was left standing on August 6, 1945 after the atomic bomb killed 200,000 people in the city. The church next door to the rectory was completely demolished by the atomic blast. There was nothing left standing on the street outside. There was, in fact, no street outside. All that, too, was completely destroyed. Only the rectory stood amidst the surrounding rubble and four Catholic priests inside survived the first atomic blast. It was because they were living the Message of Our Lady of Fatima that they were saved from certain death.[7] Indeed, Our Lady and Her Rosary are more powerful than even the atomic bomb.

• Austria 1955

There are many examples of the power of the Rosary. To give another example in our own time — the Russian armies withdrew out of Austria in 1955, without one person being killed and without one shot being fired. It is the only time that the Militant Atheistic forces of Marxism have ever peacefully left a country in which they held power. This victory for the Catholic people of Austria is due to Our Lady and Her Rosary, because at that time ten percent of the people of Austria were praying the Rosary every day. The Rosary is more powerful than guns or bombs, as we can see from this example of Austria. Through the power of the Rosary, the forces of Militant Atheism gave Austria back its freedom. God has the power to soften any human heart, as Scripture says, "The heart of the king is in the Hand of God." God, through the intercession of Our Lady, and through the prayer of the Holy Rosary, softened the hearts of the Russian rulers, and thus they gave Austria back its freedom. Sister Lucia of Fatima has said that there is no problem, either material or moral, national or international, that cannot be solved effectively by the Rosary and our sacrifices.

• Today We Need the Rosary More Than Ever

We can see from events in Poland that Communism has not changed its goal of world domination and of enslaving each one of us. Today we are all very much threatened on every side by Communism and by Militant Atheism. But the Blessed Virgin Mary can overcome these forces of evil overnight if enough people will pray the daily Rosary.

Particularly is the Family Rosary recommended, for "the family that prays together stays together", and today our families are threatened with breakup on all sides. And in this regard, Pope St. Pius X said: "The Rosary is the most beautiful and the most rich in graces of all prayers, it is the prayer that touches most the Heart of the Mother of God . . . and if you wish peace to reign in your homes, recite the family Rosary."

Regarding the family Rosary, here is what some of the other Roman Pontiffs have said: "If you desire peace in your hearts, in your homes, in your country, assemble every evening to recite the Rosary." —

Pope Pius IX

"There is no surer means of calling down God's blessings upon the family . . . than the daily recitation of the Rosary." — Pope Pius XII

"It will not then seem too much to say that . . . in families . . . in which the Rosary of Mary retains its ancient honor, the loss of faith through error and vicious ignorance need not be feared." — Pope Leo XIII

At Fatima, Our Lady asked us to recite the following prayer after each decade of the Rosary: "O my Jesus, forgive us our sins, save us from the fire of hell, lead all souls to Heaven, especially those most in need."

• **The Catholic Church Endorses the Message of Fatima**

As you recall, the Magisterium of the Roman Catholic Church has encouraged us to believe in, and to practice, the Message of Fatima, which is simply calling us to return to living the Gospel of Jesus Christ. The Bishop of Fatima authorized public promotion of devotion to Our Lady of Fatima after a most thorough, scientific and theological examination of the events of Fatima. Pope Pius XII actively promoted the Message of Fatima and was pleased to be called the Pope of Fatima. Pope John XXIII said that Fatima is the center of all Christian hopes. Pope John XXIII also said: "We exhort you to listen with simplicity of heart and honesty of mind to the salutary warnings of the Mother of God." Pope Paul VI at the Vatican council announced that he was sending the Golden Rose to Fatima.

On May 13, 1965, Pope Paul VI, through a papal

emissary, presented a Golden Rose at Fatima and, at the same time, he confided "the entire Church" to Our Lady of Fatima's protection.

He himself went there as a Pilgrim for Peace in 1967 on the 50th anniversary of Our Lady's first appearance there. He wrote an Encyclical on the occasion of his pilgrimage to Fatima. He blessed seventy National Pilgrim Statues to travel continually throughout seventy nations, so that these nations would remember and practice the message of Fatima.

Canada and the United States were blessed to be given this special grace of having a National Pilgrim Statue blessed by the Pope. Pope John Paul II is a great devotee of Our Lady. He makes continuous public profession of His personal consecration to Our Lady by His Papal coat of Arms on which is inscribed the words "Totus Tuus", that is "I am all Yours, O Mary." He, as Cardinal, twice signed petitions to the Holy Father asking the Pope to do what Our Lady of Fatima asked for — namely, that the Pope, together with all the Catholic Bishops of the world on one special day, consecrate Russia to the Immaculate Heart of Mary. He wrote:

"We believe that through this act of trustful confidence in the Mother of the Church, mankind will be saved from atheism, war and complete ruin. The Mother of God will be with you, Holy Father, and with the world for its rescue. There will arise an era of peace and victory in the cause of Christ."

Pope John Paul II wants to do as Our Lady of Fatima asked. He leads the Rosary on Vatican Radio on the First Saturday of the month. "The Rosary is my favorite prayer," Pope John Paul II said. He, himself, encourages the continuous spread of the Message of Our Lady of Fatima.

• **Fatima More Important Today Than Ever**

As we have seen in this book, the Message of Fatima and its prophecies and warnings are more important to all of us now in the 1990s than ever before. We all know that Russia in 1917 was powerless, but in 1990 is the most powerful nation in the world, and that it has enslaved one-third of the world. Our Lady predicted that all of us, everywhere in the world, will be enslaved if we do not heed Her Message of Fatima. Some people may not feel that this prediction of Fatima will happen to us here in our own country at this time. Having read this book, you can see for yourself that more than ever **we need to heed the message of Fatima** before it is too late.

The question before us now is whether you and I will heed in time Her Message, Her Maternal Appeal to us Her children, to help Her bring peace and salvation to many souls in our time. If we ignore Her, no one can, and no one will help us. If we ignore Her, God Himself will not help us because He sent His Mother to tell us what we must do to have peace and international security. If we ignore the message of Fatima, we are ignoring God's final warning, and it is certain "that many nations will be annihilated'.

Let us hope, work, and pray that this destruction of very many people and of many nations will not be necessary to awaken mankind to the fact that it is following a perilous path; that is, a path which takes us away from God and leads to self-destruction. Let us do our part. It will not be overlooked by Our Lady. Our efforts will certainly be rewarded. Each of us, personally, need not wait for our neighbor to act. Each of us, personally, will receive our own reward now and in eternity for listening to Her Maternal Message of love and concern. If enough of us in our time listen to Her, then true Christian peace will come into the whole world and Russia will be converted to the Faith of Christ, the Catholic Faith.

- **Peace Depends on You**

St. James said he who can do good and does not do it, does evil. (James 4:17) We can do good, we can bring peace to the world. We can stop the nuclear war about to start. We have the power to do it by fulfilling the simple requests of Our Lady of Fatima. It is not too hard. Will you do good? Or will you do evil? PEACE DEPENDS ON YOU!

Footnotes to Part III

6. The Blessed Virgin Mary promised Catholics who are enrolled in the Scapular of Our Lady of Mount Carmel as follows:
"Take this Scapular, whosoever dies wearing it shall not suffer eternal fire. It shall be a sign of salvation — a protection in danger and a pledge of peace." This promise was made to St. Simon Stock in 1251 in England and since that time many Popes downthrough the last seven centuries have encouraged Catholics to wear the Scapular. Pope Paul VI, explaining on February 2nd, 1965, what the Vatican Council wrote about devotion to Our Lady had these words to say: "Ever hold in great esteem the practices and exercises of devotion to the Most Holy Virgin which have been recommended for centuries by the Magisterium of the Church. And among them we judge well to recall especially the Marian Rosary and the religious use of the Scapular of Mount Carmel."

7. Father Hubert Schiffer, one of these priests, was in the rectory which was located only eight blocks from ground zero when the atom bomb exploded. More than two hundred experts have subsequently studied him, wondering how he could have survived. He answers by pointing to his Rosary. He says the message of Fatima is linked to the message of Hiroshima; Either we will pray for peace and be spared as Our Lady foretold, or we shall see even the "annihilation of entire nations".

206

Part IV — WHAT YOU CAN DO

• Remember Our Lady of Fatima's Peace Plan

Our Lady of Fatima appeared to Lucy, Jacinta and Francisco. She gave them a message to be delivered to the faithful everywhere. She told them that men must stop sinning and return to God. She told us we must pray the Rosary every day and that we must fulfill the duties of our state in life day by day.

God worked a very great miracle before more than 70,000 people at Fatima so that all people would listen to His Mother's pressing appeal. She came to Fatima out of Her maternal concern for us, Her children, but if we ignore Her, then terrible things will happen. Many souls will go to hell forever — and all of us on earth will be enslaved in a world-wide prison of Communism. If we listen — true peace will be given to the world and many souls will merit eternal happiness in Heaven.

Our Lady said: "Many souls go to hell because they have no one to pray for them and make sacrifices for them.

"If you do what I tell you many souls will be saved and there will be peace." But let us especially remember She said: "If My requests are granted, Russia will be converted and there will be peace."

"If My requests are not granted, Russia will spread its errors throughout the world raising up wars and persecutions against the Church. The good will be martyred, the Holy Father will have much to suffer — several nations will be annihilated."

Sister Lucia of Fatima was left on earth to explain the message of Our Lady of Fatima to the world. She has stated clearly that if we do not heed Our Lady's requests then Communism will enslave the whole world, including the United States.

In answer to the question: "What must the individual Catholic do in order that peace be given to the world, Communism be turned back, and the annihilation of nations be averted" Sister Lucia gave the Peace Pledge Formula, which is as follows:

Dear Queen and Mother,

Who promised at Fatima to convert Russia and bring peace to all mankind, in reparation to Your Immaculate Heart for my sins and the sins of the whole world, I solemnly promise: (1) to offer up every day the sacrifices demanded by my daily duty; (2) to say part of the Rosary (five decades) daily while meditating on the Mysteries; (3) to wear the Scapular of Mount Carmel as a profession of this promise and as an act of consecration to You. I shall renew this promise often, especially in moments of temptation.

Signature...

(This pledge is not a vow and does not bind under pain of sin. Nevertheless, it is a promise — your word given to your Heavenly Mother.)

NOTE: Baptized Catholics may be officially enrolled in the Scapular[6] to gain the promise. A non-Catholic may wear the Brown Scapular and will receive blessings for doing so.

• **Sign Our Lady of Fatima's Peace Pledge**

We urge each one of you to give your word to Our Lady that you will keep this above-mentioned peace pledge and sign your name to the pledge.

We would suggest that you send your name and address and inform us that you have signed the pledge. (But, even without sending in your name and address, you may join the Rosary Crusade by just simply giving your word to Our Lady that you will fulfill the pledge.) If you have signed the pledge already, it would be good to renew your resolution, your promise to Our Lady, and let this booklet serve as a reminder to you to keep the pledge for the rest of your life.

Of course, Our Lady would be especially pleased if, besides fulfilling Her requests as summarized in the pledge, we were to pray more and make more sacrifices as the children of Fatima did. Let us keep the five First Saturdays of Fatima and make devotion to the Immaculate Heart of Mary better known. Let us learn more about Our Lady of Fatima's teaching and always try to be as generous as possible with Our Spiritual Mother.

- **Consecrate Yourself to Our Lady's**
  Act of Consecration to the Immaculate Heart
  of Mary

O Immaculate Heart of Mary, Queen of Heaven and Earth, and tender Mother of men, in accordance with Thy ardent wish made known at Fatima, I consecrate to Thee myself, my brethren, my country, and the whole human race.

Reign over us and teach us how to make the Heart of Jesus reign and triumph in us, and around us, as It has reigned and triumphed in Thee.

Reign over us, dearest Mother, that we may be Thine in prosperity and in adversity, in joy and in sorrow, in health and in sickness, in life and in death.

O most compassionate Heart of Mary, Queen of Virgins, watch over our minds and hearts and

209

preserve them from the deluge of impurity which Thou didst lament so sorrowfully at Fatima. We want to be pure like Thee. We want to call down upon our country and the whole world the peace of God in justice and charity.

Therefore, we now promise to imitate Thy virtues by the practice of a Christian life without regard to human respect.

We resolve to receive Holy Communion regularly and to offer Thee five decades of the Rosary each day, together with our sacrifices, in the spirit of reparation and penance. Amen.

• Block Rosary

We also urge you to form a Block Rosary group in your area with your friends and neighbors. Gather in one of your homes at the same time each week to pray the Rosary for our country. Let us also pray for our Bishops and the Pope, so that they do their part to bring peace to the world by consecrating Russia to the Immaculate Heart of Mary in the form that God requested through Our Lady of Fatima. Keep this Block Rosary spiritual and simple by meeting only to pray the Rosary. Do not serve refreshments or have discussions or long conversations on these occasions. It is not a social event. Do not let the Block Rosary in your area lose its spiritual purpose little by little by letting it turn into a social event.

You and your friends may also try to meet in your local Parish Church at the same time each week to pray the Rosary for peace in our country and peace in the world. Before you do this, of course, ask your Parish Priest for permission to pray aloud the Rosary in Church, as it may happen that something else is scheduled for the hour you have chosen.

Many parishes have introduced the practice of praying out loud the Rosary before each Mass on weekdays and on Sundays. You, or a Parish group, could ask your Pastor to allow you to introduce this practice in your parish.

• **Peace Plan for Canada and the U.S.A.**

Undertake today to do your part by signing and keeping the Peace Pledge Formula as indicated by Our Lady of Fatima to Sister Lucy, and establish the saying of the Rosary once a week with a group of friends for the special intention of saving Canada and the United States from the plans of the devil and the Militant Atheists in our midst.

• **Constant Vigil of Prayer**

As well as praying the daily Rosary, we urge you to set aside fifteen minutes or an hour each week to pray the Rosary with your family or alone, in Church or at home, to pray the Rosary so that God will bring peace to our country and the world.

We encourage you to send in a note to the Fatima Rosary Crusade headquarters to inform us of the hour and day that you will be saying the Rosary for peace in our country and the world. By means of this information, we will be able to help you and others organize a constant vigil of prayer across our country so that in every area there will be many prayers ascending to God and the Blessed Virgin Mary throughout the 168 hours of the week calling down God's blessing and protection on our people and land.

- **Pass On This Information**

We also urge you to pass on this booklet to your friends, relatives and acquaintances; give a copy to everyone you talk to, and talk about it in conversations. Enclose a copy with every letter you write, and send a copy to all on your Christmas card list. Bring copies to distribute and to read at every meeting you attend. Get your civic and religious groups to undertake to promote the Rosary as one of their projects. Ask your group to help you distribute this booklet. Extra copies are available from the publisher of this book.

Have this section II reprinted in its entirety, all at once, or in serial form, in your bulletins, newsletters, magazines and newspapers. You may reprint it entirely if you change nothing, and include the address, giving "The Fatima Rosary Crusade" credit for the article.

You might especially try to bring this booklet to the attention of groups such as the C.W.L., Knights of Columbus, Legion of Mary, Pro-Life Groups, your Marian and Fatima groups, Third Orders, local unions and professional associations, political groups. Take it to work; give copies to co-workers, customers and clients. Pass it on to religious magazines and newspapers; ask them to reprint it.

We need your help to pass the word on to your friends and neighbors, and if you can, any financial assistance — donations sent to our headquarters will be used to pay for the printing and other expenses of continuing the Fatima Rosary Crusade.

Saints and the Rosary

"One day through the Rosary and Scapular I will save the world".

... Prophecy of Our Lady to St. Dominic.

"If, by the grace of God, you have already reached a high level of prayer, keep up the practice of saying the Holy Rosary if you wish to remain in that state and if you hope to grow in humility. For never will anyone who says the Rosary every day become a formal heretic or be led astray by the devil. This is a statement that I would gladly sign with my blood." St. Louis de Montfort

Our Lady of Fatima's
"Great Promise" of Aid for Salvation

"I promise to help at the hour of death, with the graces needed for their salvation whosoever on the first Saturday of five consecutive months shall confess and receive Holy Communion, recite five decades of the Rosary and keep Me company for 15 minutes while meditating on the 15 mysteries of the Rosary with the intention of making Reparation to Me."

Footnotes to Part IV

6. The Blessed Virgin Mary promised Catholics who are enrolled in the Scapular of Our Lady of Mount Carmel as follows:
"Take this Scapular, whosoever dies wearing it shall not suffer eternal fire. It shall be a sign of salvation — a protection in danger and a pledge of peace." This promise was made to St. Simon Stock in 1251 in England and since that time many Popes down through the last seven centuries have encouraged Catholics to wear the Scapular. Pope Paul VI, explaining on February 2nd, 1965, what the Vatican Council wrote about devotion to Our Lady had these words to say: "Ever hold in great esteem the practices and exercises of devotion to the Most Holy Virgin which have been recommended for centuries by the Magisterium of the Church. And among them we judge well to recall especially the Marian Rosary and the religious use of the Scapular of Mount Carmel."

213

Section III

Our Lady
Of Fatima's Most
Important Request

The information in this section is also available from:
The Fatima Crusader

In **U.S.A.:** P.O. Box 93
Constable, NY 12926

In **Canada:** 452 Kraft Road
Fort Erie, Ontario L2A 4M7

In **Philippines:** P.O. Box 1395
Metro, Manila 1099 - Philippines

In **India:** 6 R.R. Flats, Anthu Street,
Santhome, Madras 600 004 - South India

For 10 extra copies there is no donation expected.

For more copies please send sufficient amount to cover
the cost of printing and postage.

Already over hundreds of thousands have been
distributed.

It is also available in the Portuguese language.

Section III

OUR LADY OF FATIMA'S MOST IMPORTANT REQUEST

Remember: Our Lady of Fatima said: "I shall come to ask for the Consecration of Russia to My Immaculate Heart . . . If My requests are not granted, Russia will spread its errors throughout the world raising up wars and persecutions against the Church. The good will be martyred, the Holy Father will have much to suffer. Various nations will be annihilated."

Sister Lucy has confirmed that if we do not heed the Message of Fatima in time, the whole world including the United States of America will be scourged and enslaved by Communist Russia.

In the name of Jesus, in 1929 Our Lady did return to ask for this most important act of obedience by the Pope and the bishops. She said: "The moment has come for God to ask the Holy Father to make in union with all the bishops of the world, the consecration of Russia to My Immaculate Heart. He promises to save Russia **BY THIS MEANS** . . . Sacrifice yourself for this intention and pray."

Referring to this command to consecrate Russia, Jesus said to Sister Lucia of Fatima; "Make it known to My ministers that given that they follow the example of the King of France in delaying the execution of My Command, they will follow him into misfortune."They have not wished to listen to My Command.

Like the King of France, they will repent of this and they will do it, but it will be late. Russia will have already spread her errors throughout the world provoking wars and persecutions against the Church. The Holy Father will have much to suffer."

The Pope, together with all the Catholic bishops on the exact same day must solemnly and publicly consecrate specifically RUSSIA to the Immaculate Heart of Mary. Pope John Paul II wants to obey this command but he needs your support. Both Pope John Paul II and Sister Lucia agree, the Consecration of Russia has not yet been done as Our Lady of Fatima has commanded.

Remember that it is only "BY THIS MEANS" that Russia will be converted and peace given to the world. And that if Our Lady's requests are not obeyed in time then "many nations will disappear from the face of the earth", "annihilated."

Sister Lucia asked Jesus why He would not convert Russia without the Pope making the Consecration of Russia together with all the bishops. Jesus replied: "because I want My whole church to acknowledge that Consecration as a triumph of the Immaculate Heart of Mary." Our Lady at Fatima said, "God wishes to establish in the world Devotion to My Immaculate Heart."

In 1992, we, too, can all KNOW that this command to consecrate Russia has not been done because Russia has clearly not been converted. Thus you can see that your lives, your possessions, your freedom, your souls are in grave danger because the command given by God to the Pope and the bishops through Our Lady of Fatima HAS NOT YET BEEN HEEDED.

Do your part. Our Holy Father, Pope John Paul II needs your support. He wants to make the consecration but we **MUST** show him we are behind him. SIGN THIS PETITION NOW and send it to the Pope via the Militia of Our Immaculate Mother, Box 602, Fort Erie, Ontario, Canada L2A 5X3 or 85 Allen Street, Suite 505, Buffalo, NY 14202. (Extra copies of this petition in the box below are found at the end of this book). Make as many copies of this petition as possible and collect more signatures. The time is now. You must act now before it is too late.

Dear Holy Father,
Please, we beg you, protect us from the horrors of Militant Atheism headquartered in Russia. Help us preserve our homes, our freedom and help us to save our souls. **Consecrate Russia** to the Immaculate Heart of Mary now as Our Lord requested through the Message of Fatima. We offer our prayers and sacrifices to help you achieve this purpose. God Bless you and Our Lady protect you.

Signed _____

Remember, Jesus said to Sister Lucia: "Pray a great deal for the Holy Father. He will do it (the consecration of Russia together with all the Catholic Bishops) but it will be late."

Sister Lucia herself said: "Tell them Father, that many times, the Most Holy Virgin told my cousins Francisco and Jacinta, as well as myself, that many nations will disappear from the face of the earth. She said that Russia will be the instrument of chastisement chosen by Heaven to punish the whole world if we do not beforehand obtain the conversion of that poor nation."

Section IV

The Plans of Christ the King for True World Peace,

Contrasted Against

The Plans of Satan for World Tyranny and Destruction

by
Father Denis Fahey C.S.Sp.

Introduction to Section IV

You must do your part to Help Bring About Our Lady's Triumph And Period Of Peace by being more fully informed about the Reign of Christ the King.

Our Lady of Fatima promised: "In the end My Immaculate Heart will Triumph, The Holy Father will Consecrate Russia to Me, Russia will be converted and a period of peace will be given to mankind."

In today's world we must be careful to understand the words of Our Lady as She intended them to be understood. The secular media, the organ of the secular humanist religion, through their own reports, editorialize analyses and distort the news and entertainment to accommodate their basic lie that Jesus Christ and the Blessed Virgin Mary have nothing much to do with world peace or peace in our communities and our homes.

Their words lie if not explicitly, at least implicitly. It is obvious that God and the one true Religion of Jesus Christ and the Blessed Virgin Mary are never or almost never mentioned in the secular media. By that fact alone all the news they give us is biased because God has everything to do with our lives and our peace.

But often in the secular media even single facts are distorted to give a very different picture to the general public from what is actually going on.

Even Catholic papers are infected with naturalism and secularism when it comes to reporting news of world events. When they do introduce the supernatural into it, it is often distorted to such a degree that the truth is not recognizable. A recent example of this is the so-called "Conversion of Russia" that some naive commentators imply or state when they report about the Berlin Wall, Glasnost, Perestroika and the "Coup" of August 1991 in Moscow.

So as not to be deceived by those who conspire against God and man, or by those willing accomplices working for money, power or prestige, or who simply do it out of total ignorance of the two armed and opposing camps - that of Jesus Christ and His Most Holy Mother against that of satan and his followers, we present below the outline of the plans and programs of these two camps - which you, willingly or not, are destined to take the side of satan if you do not take the side of Christ.

We especially must not be deceived by those Catholics who promote satan's "New World Order". They think they are performing a service to Jesus Christ and His Church. If you question them, they would claim it is what Pope John Paul himself is promoting. God forbid! We hope this is not true. The "New World Order" is against God, His Church and His plan for real World Order and Peace.

St. Robert Bellarmine, Doctor of the Church, a staunch defender of the Papacy, tells us that we must resist efforts of anyone, including a Priest, Bishop, Cardinal, and even a Pope who would attack the faith, or pursue policies that would endanger the Catholic Faith - even if they do it with good intentions as for example through ignorance and lack of prudence.

St. Thomas Aquinas and other Doctors of the Church agree with St. Robert Bellarmine. The reason is clear, the faith is the foundation of our salvation. Without the Catholic Faith we cannot save our souls. Therefore, if we do not defend the Faith when it is attacked, there is great danger souls will be lost because they abandon the faith. St. Paul gave us the perfect example in his epistle to the Galations of defending the Faith against the first Pope. When St. Peter, for diplomatic reasons, was "not standing in the truth," St. Paul publicly rebuked him. St. Peter corrected himself.

In these confusing times it is important for us to realize that Jesus Christ is "King of kings and Lord of lords," and He does not expect only to be honoured in correct liturgical services...

No, Our Lord and Saviour expects kings, rulers, ministers, senators, legislators, presidents, supreme court justices, citizens, electors and jurors, etc., to give public witness and public expression in the social institutions, courts, hospitals, schools, government agencies, etc. - to the Law of Jesus Christ. In fact, there will be no peace until the rule of law of the Prince of Peace - Jesus Christ is recognized by society in communities, courtrooms, local governments, national government and international law and diplomacy. Our Lady of Fatima promised a period of peace to mankind. This means that the plans of Jesus Christ for world order will be implemented in the Reign of Peace She promised.

St. Thomas Aquinas defines peace as the "tranquillity of order." The only order that will really achieve this tranquillity is the order established by Our Creator and Redeemer. The only way for us to have peace is to follow the order, the plan of God for World Order - not a "New World Order" (N.W.O.) - but the Order God has planned and decreed for mankind, since He promised a Redeemer to all in the first book of the Bible. This order must give sincere public recognition to Jesus Christ Our King and Mary

Our Immaculate Queen. Remember God promised to send the Woman (Genesis 3:15) Who would crush the serpent's (satan's) head. The same woman was predicted to us in the Apocalypse (12:1). The Woman clothed with the Sun. That same woman prophesied, has now come clothed with the Sun at Fatima and promised to triumph over satan and his followers. "In the end My Immaculate Heart will triumph." But She wants us to join in the battle and to do so intelligently. That is why we present below the two plans - so you can recognize in your everyday decisions which plan to advance and which to retard. You must do your part to be a peacemaker. It is your duty before God and man.

Remember the peace and the order of the world must be based on Jesus' Law and must repudiate satan's plan for organizing the world and society. Since many people of good will do not know the outline of Christ's plan, and since many are unwittingly helping satan impose or maintain his stranglehold on society, we present here the two opposing plans for human society - so you can help Jesus Christ advance His plans here on earth, and you can do all you can to retard the plans of satan.

Publishers Note: The above introduction to Section IV is by the publisher of this book. The work of Father Fahey starts on page 227 and the subtitles in this section by Father Fahey were added by the publisher.

THE PROGRAM OF CHRIST CONTRASTED AGAINST THE PLANS OF SATAN

Our Lord's Program for Order may be outlined as follows:

The Role of the Catholic Church

Our Lord's Mystical Body, the Catholic Church, Supernatural and Supranational, which all States and Nations are called upon to acknowledge, has been established by God as the One Way for the ordered return of human beings to Him. Into it all men of all Nations are called to enter as His Members. "Men living together in society are under the power of God no less than individuals are, and society, not less than individuals, owes gratitude to God, Who gave it being and maintains it, and Whose ever-bounteous goodness enriches it with countless blessings. Since, then, no one is allowed to be remiss in the service due

Satan's Plans for Disorder may be outlined as follows:

Satan's Plans Against the Church

Satan aims at preventing the acknowledgment by States and Nations of the Catholic Church as the One Way established by God for ordered return to Him. When this acknowledgment has been brought about in spite of his efforts and those of his satellites, he strives to get it undone and to induce the State to persecute the Catholic Church. The first step towards this is to get all religions, including the Jewish religion, put on the same level as the Catholic Church. The granting of full citizenship to the Jews, who, *as a nation*, are engaged in preparing for the natural Messias, tends in the same direction. This putting of all religions on the same level is usually

to God. . . *we are bound absolutely to worship God in that way which He has shown to be His will.* . . It cannot be difficult to find out which is the true religion, if only it be sought with an earnest and unbiased mind; for proofs are abundant and striking. . . From all these *[proofs]* it is evident that the only true religion is the one established by Jesus Christ Himself, and which He committed to His Church to protect and propagate" (Leo XIII, Encyclical Letter, *Immortale Dei, On the Christian Constitution of States).*

"Justice therefore forbids, and reason itself forbids, the State to be godless; or to adopt a line of action which would end in godlessness — namely, to treat the various religions (as they call them) alike, and *to bestow upon them promiscuously equal rights and privileges.* Since, then, the profession of one religion is necessary in the State, that religion must be professed which alone is true, and which can be recog-

called in the newspapers *separation of Church and State.* (Cf. Accounts of Revolutions from the French Revolution of 1789 to the Spanish Revolution of 1931).

Satan spreads perplexity and disorder in minds by confusing the false *tolerance of Liberalism*, by which equal rights are granted to truth and error, with the true *tolerance* of the Catholic Church. "As to tolerance," writes Leo XIII (Encyclical Letter, *Libertas, On Human Liberty*), "it is surprising how far removed from the equity and prudence of the Church are those who profess what is called Liberalism. For, in allowing that boundless license of which We have spoken, they exceed all limits and end at last by making no apparent distinction between truth and error, honesty and dishonesty... *it is contrary to reason that error and truth should have equal rights.* . . For right is a moral

nized without difficulty, especially in Catholic States, because the marks of truth are, as it were, engraven upon it" (Leo XIII, Encyclical Letter, *Libertas, On Human Liberty*).

"By degrees the religion of Christ was put on the same level with false religions and placed ignominiously in the same category with them" (Pius XI, Encyclical Letter, *Quas Primas, On the Kingship of Christ*).

Pope Pius XI condemned separation of Church and State more than once. In the Encyclical, *On Christian Marriage*, he praised the Italian Matrimonial Law and the solemn Convention entered into between the Holy See and the Kingdom of Italy and then added: "This might well be a striking example to all of how, even in this our own day (in which, sad to say, the absolute separation of the civil power from the Church, and indeed from every religion, is so often taught), the one supreme authority can be united and associated with the other without detriment to the rights and supreme

power which it is absurd to suppose that nature has accorded indifferently to truth and falsehood, justice and injustice."

"The Church," writes the same learned Pontiff (Encyclical Letter, *Immortale Dei, On the Christian Constitution of States*), "deems it unlawful to place the various forms of divine worship on the same footing as the true religion, but does not on that account, condemn those rulers, who for the sake of securing some great good or of hindering some great evil, patiently allow custom or usage to be a kind of sanction for each kind of religion having its place in the State. And, in fact, the Church is wont to take earnest heed that no one shall be forced to embrace the Catholic Faith against his will."

Satan also spreads perplexity and disorder in minds by introducing confusion between Anti-Semitism, which is the detestable hatred of the

(Our Lord's Program)	(Satan's Aims)

power of either, thus protecting Christian parents from pernicious evils and menacing ruin."

Again the same Pontiff writes as follows: "It is assuredly with no small grief We learn that the legislators have openly declared that the State has no religion, and that they have accordingly confirmed and ratified what the Constitution of the Spanish Government has already unjustly laid down, namely, the separation of Civil Society from the Church. To avoid dwelling too long on this matter, We do not wish to point out at too great length *what a grievous error they commit who hold that such a separation is licit and worthy of approval*, especially since it is a question of a nation almost all of whose citizens glory in the name of Catholic. Indeed, if the matter is examined closely, this iniquitous separation, as We have more than once indicated, is the necessary consequence of the theories of the Laicists" (Encyclical Letter, *On the Persecution of the Church in Spain*).

Pope Leo XIII stressed

Jews as a race, and the duty incumbent upon Catholics of combating valiantly for the integral rights of Christ the King and opposing Jewish Naturalism. We see this clearly in the following quotation from the Jewish writer Bernard Lazare: "The Jew is the living testimony of the disappearance of the State based on theological principles, that state which the Anti-Semites hope to restore. From the day a Jew first occupied a public position, the Christian State was in danger. That is perfectly accurate and the Anti-Semites who say that the Jews have destroyed the correct idea of the State could more justly assert that the entrance of the Jews into Christian Society has symbolized the destruction of the State, I mean, of course, the Christian State" (*L'Anti-sémitisme, p. 361*).

Satan wants us to forget that there is one True Religion, the Supernatural

the same divine principle. "The main factor in bringing things to this happy state were the ordinances and decrees of your synods, especially of those which in more recent times were convened and confirmed by the authority of the Apostolic See. But, moreover (a fact which it gives pleasure to acknowledge), thanks are due to the equity of the laws which obtain in America and to the customs of your well-ordered Republic. For the Church amongst you, unopposed by the Constitution and government of your nation, fettered by no hostile legislation, protected against violence by the common laws and the impartiality of the tribunals, is free to live and act without hindrance. Yet, though all this is true, it would be very erroneous to draw the conclusion that in America is to be sought the type of the most desirable status of the Church, or that it would be universally lawful or expedient for State and Church to be, as in America, separated and divorced." (Encyclical Letter, *Longinque Oceani, On Catholicity*

Religion established by Our Lord Jesus Christ, True God and True Man. He wants us also to lose sight of the fact that there are organized forces working for the advent of the Natural Messias.

"*By the fact that the indiscriminate freedom of all forms of worship is proclaimed,* truth is confused with error, and the Holy and Immaculate Spouse of Christ is placed on the same level as heretical sects and even as Jewish perfidy" (Pius VII, Letter, *Post tam diuturnas*).

Satan has not left us in doubt about his enthusiasm for the Declaration of the "rights of man" and the principles of the French Revolution of 1789. "Long live Liberty, Equality, Fraternity! That is the favorable time for us" are amongst the expressions used by the possessed children of Illfurt, Alsace. (*Cf. The devil, his words and actions in the possessed children of Illfurt,* from the official

(Our Lord's Program)	(Satan's Aims)

in the United States).

documents).

Relationship of Nations to the Catholic Church

And as a consequence, States and Nations are called upon to acknowledge the right of the Catholic Church by the voice of the Pope and Bishops to decide what favors or hinders our most real life, namely, our life as Members of Christ. This right of the Catholic Church is known as the *Indirect Power*. It belongs to the Catholic Church as the sole divinely-appointed Guardian of the whole Moral Law, natural and revealed.

"The Church of Christ is the true and sole teacher of virtue and guardian of morals" (Leo XIII, Encyclical Letter, *Immortale Dei, On the Christian Constitution of States*).

"The Lord Jesus reigns in *civil society*. . . when the Church holds that position of dignity which was allotted to her by her Divine Author, that of a perfect society, mistress and guide of all other societies" (Pope Pius XI, Encyclical Letter, *Ubi Arcano, On the Peace of Christ in the Kingdom of Christ*).

"If the natural law en-

Satan's Attack on Nations Right to Hear the Church

Satan aims at getting States and Nations to treat with contempt the Indirect Power of the Catholic Church and at setting up the State or the Race as the authority to decide all moral questions. He knows that this means the abrogation of the moral law and that it leads to chaos.

"To create this atmosphere of lasting peace, neither peace treaties nor the most solemn pacts, nor international meetings or conferences, nor even the noblest and most disinterested efforts of any statesman will be enough, unless in the first place are recognized the sacred rights of natural and divine law. No leader in public economy, no power of organization will ever be able to bring social conditions to a peaceful solution, unless the moral law, based on God and conscience, first triumphs in the field of economics itself. This is the

joins upon us to love devotedly and to defend the country that gave us birth, and in which we were brought up, so that every good citizen hesitates not to face death for his native land, very much more is it the urgent duty of Christians to be ever animated by like sentiments towards the Church. For the Church is the Holy City of the Living God, born of God Himself, and by Him built up and established. Therefore we are bound to love dearly the country whence we have received the means of enjoyment this mortal life affords, but we have a much more urgent obligation to love, with ardent love, the Church to which we owe the life of the soul, a life that will endure forever" (Leo XIII, Encyclical Letter, *Sapientiæ Christianæ On the Chief Duties of Christians as Citizens*). "Christ instituted in the Church a *living, authoritative and permanent Teaching Authority*, which He strengthened by His own power, taught by the Spirit of Truth, and confirmed by miracles. He willed and ordered, under the gravest penalties, that its teachings should be received as if they were His own" (Leo

underlying value of every value in the political life as well as in the economic life of nations" (Pius XI, Encyclical Letter, *Caritate Christi Compulsi, On the Troubles of Our Time*).

"He who takes the race, or the people, or the State, or the form of Government, the bearers of the power of the State or other fundamental elements of human society — which in the temporal order of things have an essential and honorable place — out of the system of their earthly valuation and makes them the ultimate norm of all, even of religious values, and deifies them with an idolatrous worship, perverts and falsifies the order of things created and commanded by God" (Pius XI, *The Persecution of the Church in Germany*).

Lured on by satan, men talk of restoring order in the world in defiance of or without the help of Christ and His Church. This will only lead to greater chaos: "No human institution exists which can impose upon

XIII, Encyclical Letter, *Satis Cognitum, On the Unity of the Church*).

"In defining the limits of the obedience owed to the pastors of souls," writes Pope Leo XIII, "but most of all to the authority of the Roman Pontiff, it must not be supposed that it is only to be yielded in relation to dogmas of which the obstinate denial cannot be disjoined from the crime of heresy. Nay further, it is not enough sincerely and firmly to assent to doctrines which, though not defined by any solemn pronouncement of the Church, are by her proposed to belief, as divinely revealed in her common and universal teaching and which the Vatican Council declared are to be believed with Catholic and divine faith.

"But this likewise must be reckoned amongst the duties of Christians, that they allow themselves to be ruled and directed by the authority and leadership of their bishops, and above all of the Apostolic See. . . Wherefore it belongs to the Pope to judge authoritatively what things the sacred oracles contain, as well as what doctrines are in harmony, and what in disagreement,

the nations an international code, adapted to the present time, similar to the one which in the Middle Ages, ruled that society of nations which was known as Christendom. . . But there is a divine institution, which can guarantee the sanctity of the law of nations, an institution which embracing all nations and transcending them, is endowed with supreme authority and evokes veneration through its plenary powers of rule — the Church of Christ" (Pius XI, Encyclical Letter, *Ubi Arcano, On the Peace of Christ in the Kingdom of Christ*).

Satan tries to persuade young people that the Church is opposed to the form of civil government they prefer. This is not true. "Of the various governments, the Church does not reject any that are fitted to procure the welfare of the subject; she wishes only — and this nature itself requires — that they should be constituted without involving wrong to anyone

with them; and also for the same reason to show forth what things are to be accepted as right, and what to be rejected as worthless; what it is necessary to do and what to avoid doing, in order to attain eternal salvation. For otherwise, there would be no sure interpreter of the commands of God, nor would there be any safe guide showing man the way he should live. . . From God has the duty been assigned to the Church not only to interpose resistance, if at times the State rule should run counter to religion, but, further, to make a strong endeavor that the power of the Gospel may pervade the laws and institutions of the nations. And inasmuch as the destiny of the State depends mainly on the disposition of those who are at the head of affairs, it follows that the Church cannot give countenance or favor to those whom she knows to be imbued with a spirit of hostility to her, who refuse openly to respect her rights; who make it their aim and purpose to tear asunder the alliance that should, by the very nature of things, connect the interests of religion with those of the State. On the contrary, she is (as she

and especially without violating the rights of the Church" (Leo XIII, Encyclical Letter, *Libertas, On Human Liberty*).

He tries to persuade them also that the Catholic Church is opposed to all efforts for a country's independence. This also is false. "Neither does the Church condemn those who, if it can be done without violation of justice, wish to make their country independent of any foreign or despotic power. Nor does she blame those who wish to secure to the State the power of self-government, and to its citizens the greatest possible measure of prosperity" (Leo XIII, Encyclical Letter, *Libertas, On Human Liberty*).

The Church, of course, condemns all secret societies which are satan's happy hunting grounds: "As Our Predecessors have many times repeated, *let no man think that he may for any reason whatsoever join the Masonic sect*, if he values his Catholic name and his eternal salvation as

(Our Lord's Program)	(Satan's Aims)

is bound to be) the upholder of those who are themselves imbued with the right way of thinking as to the relations between Church and State, and who strive to make them work in perfect accord for the common good. These precepts contain the abiding principle by which every Catholic should shape his conduct in regard to public life" (Leo XIII, Encyclical Letter, *Sapientiæ Christianæ, On the Chief Duties of Christians as Citizens*).

he ought to value them. Let no one be deceived by a pretense of honesty. It may seem to some that Freemasons demand nothing that is openly contrary to religion and morality; but, as the whole principle and object of the sect lies in what is vicious and criminal, to join with these men or in any way to help them cannot be lawful" (Leo XIII, Encyclical Letter, *Humanum Genus, On Freemasonry*).

Christian Family Life

The Unity and Indissolubility of Christian Marriage symbolize the union of Christ and His Mystical Body. This is the foundation of the Christian Family. Our Lord wants His members to cultivate purity and honor virginity, under the guidance of His Immaculate Mother.

"If we wish with all reverence to inquire into the intimate reason of the divine decree (of the indissolubility of marriage), we shall easily see it in the mystical signification of Christian Marriage. . . For, as the Apostle

Satan's Plan to Undermine Family Life

Satan aims at undermining Christian family life, directly by the introduction of divorce and indirectly by the propagation of immorality. The attack on the moral law may be launched under the pretext of the interests of the race. Satan hates the pure, especially the Immaculate Queen of Heaven.

"Oh! if only your country [the United States] had come to know from the experience of others, rather than from examples at home, of the accumulation of ills which derive from

(Our Lord's Program)	(Satan's Aims)

(Our Lord's Program)

says in his Epistle to the Ephesians (V. 32), the marriage of Christians recalls that most perfect union which exists between Christ and the Church, which union, as long as Christ shall live and the Church through Him, can never be dissolved by any separation. . . "God wishes men to be born not only that they may live and fill the earth, but much more that they may be worshippers of God, that they may know Him and love Him and finally enjoy Him for ever in Heaven; and this end, since man is raised by God in a marvellous way to the supernatural order, surpasses all that eye hath seen, and ear heard, and all that hath entered into the heart of man. From which it is easily seen how great a gift of divine goodness and how remarkable a fruit of marriage are children born by the omnipotent power of God through the co-operation of those bound in wedlock.

"But Christian parents must also understand that they are destined not only to propagate and preserve the

(Satan's Aims)

the plague of divorce!. . . The consequences of this evil have been thus described by Pope Leo XIII in words whose truth cannot be gainsaid: 'Because of divorce the nuptial contract becomes subject to fickle whim; affection is weakened; pernicious incentives are given to conjugal infidelity; the care and education of offspring are harmed; the seeds of discord are sown among families, the dignity of woman is lessened and brought down, and she runs the risk of being deserted after she has served her husband as an instrument of pleasure. And since it is true that for the ruin of the family and the undermining of the State, nothing is so powerful as the corruption of morals, it is easy to see that divorce is most injurious to the prosperity of families and of States' (Encyclical Letter, *Arcanum*). . . Marriages, in which one or the other party does not accept the Catholic teaching or has not been baptized, as is clear to you from wide experience, are rarely happy and usual-

human race on earth, indeed not only to educate any kind of worshippers of the true God, but children who are to become members of the Church of Christ, to raise up fellow-citizens of the Saints, and members of God's household that the worshippers of God and Our Savior may daily increase. . . It is theirs to offer their offspring to the Church in order that by this most fruitful Mother of the children of God, they may be regenerated through the laver of Baptism unto supernatural justice and finally be made living Members of Christ, partakers of immortal life, and heirs of that eternal glory to which we all aspire from our inmost heart. . .

"All these things, however, Venerable Brethren, depend in large measure on the due preparation, remote and proximate, of the parties for marriage. For it cannot be denied that the basis of a happy wedlock, and the ruin of an unhappy one, is prepared and set in the souls of boys and girls during the period of childhood and adolescence. There is danger

ly occasion grave loss to the Catholic Church" (Pius XII, Encyclical Letter to the American Hierarchy, 1939).

"The Naturalists and Freemasons, having no faith in those things which we have learned by the revelation of God, deny that our first parents sinned, and consequently think that free will is not at all weakened and inclined to evil. . . Wherefore we see that men are publicly tempted by the many allurements of pleasure; that there are journals and pamphlets with neither moderation nor shame; that stageplays are remarkable for license; that designs for works of art are shamelessly sought in the laws of *so-called realism*; that the contrivances for a soft and delicate life are most carefully devised; and that all the allurements of pleasure by which virtue may be lulled to sleep are diligently brought into play" (Leo XIII, Encyclical Letter, *Humanum Genus, On Freemasonry*).

Satan rejoices at efforts to encourage illegitimacy, on the plea of the needs of

that those who before marriage sought in all things what was theirs, who indulged even their impure desires, will be in the married state what they were before, that they will reap that which they have sown; indeed within the home there will be sadness, lamentation, mutual contempt, strifes, estrangements, weariness of common life and, worst of all, such parties will find them- selves left alone with their own unconquered passions. Let, then, those who are about to enter on married life approach that state well disposed and well prepared, so that they will be able, as far as they can, to help each other in sustaining the vicissitudes of life, and yet more in attending to their eternal salvation and in forming the inner man unto the fullness of the age of Christ. . . The religious character of marriage, its sublime signification of grace and the union between Christ and the Church, evidently requires that those about to marry should show a holy reverence towards it, and

the race, and at efforts to corrupt the young. "Every use of the faculty given by God for the procreation of new life is the right and the privilege of the marriage state alone, by the law of God and of nature, and must be confined absolutely within the sacred limits of that state. . . For now, alas, not secretly nor under cover, but openly, with all sense of shame put aside, now by word, again by writings, by theatrical productions of every kind, by romantic fiction, by amorous and frivolous novels, by cinematographs portraying in vivid scene, in addresses broadcast on the radio, in short, by all the inventions of modern science, the sanctity of marriage is trampled upon and derided; divorce, adultery, all the basest vices either are extolled or at least are depicted in such colors as to appear to be free of all reproach and infamy. Books are not lacking which. . . to the number of antiquated opinions, relegate the traditional doctrine of Christian marriage. These thoughts are instilled into men of every

zealously endeavor to make their marriage approach as nearly as possible to the arche-type of Christ and the Church. They, therefore, who rashly and heedlessly contract mixed marriages, from which the maternal love and providence of the Church dissuades her children for very sound reasons, fail conspicuously in this respect, sometimes with danger to their eternal salvation" (Pius XI, Encyclical Letter, *Casti Connubii, On Christian Marriage*).

Christian Education

Our Lord wants children educated as Members of His Mystical Body, so that they may be able to look at everything, nationality included, from that standpoint, and observe the order following therefrom in relation to God, themselves and others. Thus is true personality developed.

"For the mere fact that a school gives some religious instruction (often extremely stinted), does not bring it into accord with the rights of the Church and of the

class, rich and poor, masters and workers, lettered and unlettered, married and single, the godly and the godless, old and young, but for these last, as easiest prey, the worst snares are laid" (Pius XI, Encyclical Letter, *Casti Connubii, On Christian Marriage*).

Satan's Plans to Destroy Christian Education

Satan aims at impeding, or if possible, preventing altogether, the education of young people of both sexes as Members of Christ. He will favor the Lutheran sectioning off of the Christian from the Citizen (or National) and will endeavor to get educators to strive for success in examinations or in games irrespective of the ordered formation of Christ's Members. He will endeavor to get Catholics thus badly educated into Secret Societies, such as Freemasonry, in order to

Christian family, or make it a fit place for Catholic students. To be this, it is necessary that all the teaching and the whole organization of the school and its teachers, syllabus and textbooks in every branch, be regulated by the Christian spirit, under the direction and maternal supervision of the Church; so that Religion may be in very truth the foundation and crown of the youth's entire training; and this in every grade of school, not only the elementary, but the intermediate and higher institutions of learning as well. To use the words of Leo XIII: 'It is necessary not only that religious instruction be given to the young at fixed times, but also that every other subject taught, be permeated with Christian piety. If this is wanting, if this sacred atmosphere does not pervade and warm the hearts of masters and scholars alike, little good can be expected from any kind of learning, and considerable harm will often be the consequence. . .'" (Encyclical Letter, *Militantis Ecclesiæ Aug. 1,*

give them a naturalistic formation and induce them to turn against the Religious Orders of the Catholic Church and against Catholic Education generally.

Satan uses every effort to lower the ideals of future priests and educators and to corrupt the future mothers of families: "Let us spread vice broadcast among the multitude. Let them breathe it through their five senses, let them drink it in and become saturated with it. . . Make men's hearts corrupt and vicious and you will have no more Catholics. Draw away priests from their work, from the altar and from the practise of virtue. Strive skillfully to fill their minds and occupy their time with other matters. . . Recently one of our friends, laughing at our projects, said to us: 'To overcome the Catholic Church, you must begin by suppressing the female sex.' There is a certain sense in which the words are true; but since we cannot suppress woman, let us corrupt her along with the Church. . . The best poniard with which to wound the Church mortally

241

(Our Lord's Program)	(Satan's Aims)

1897)", (Pope Pius XI, Encyclical Letter, *Divini Illius Magistri, On the Christian Education of Youth*).

"When one thinks of the havoc wrought in the souls of youth and of childhood, of the loss of innocence so often suffered in the motion picture theatres, there comes to mind the terrible condemnation pronounced by Our Lord upon the corrupters of little ones: 'Whosoever shall scandalize one of these little ones who believe in Me, it were better for him that a millstone be hanged about his neck and that he be drowned in the depths of the sea' (St. Matth. XVIII, 6). . . From time to time, the bishops will do well to remind the motion picture industry that, amid the cares of their pastoral ministry, they are under obligation to interest themselves in every form of decent and healthy recreation, because they are responsible before God for the moral welfare of their people even during their time of leisure. . . . Above all, all pastors of souls will undertake to obtain each year from their

is corruption" (Instructions of the Italian Masonic *Alta Vendita* in *L'Eglise Romaine en face de la Revolution*, by Crétineau-Joly, Vol. II, pp. 128-129).

"Everyone knows what damage is done to the soul by bad motion pictures. They are occasions of sin, they seduce young people along the ways of evil by glorifying the passions; they show life under a false light; they cloud ideals; they destroy pure love, respect for marriage, affection for the family. . . The power of the motion picture consists in this, that it speaks by means of vivid and concrete imagery which the mind takes in with enjoyment and without fatigue. . . This power is still greater in the talking picture for the reason that interpretation becomes even easier and the charm of music is added to the action of the drama. . . It is therefore one of the supreme necessities of our times to watch and to labor to the end that the motion picture be no longer a school of corruption but that it be transformed into an effectual instrument for the education and the eleva-

people a pledge similar to the one already alluded to, which is given by their American brothers and in which they promise to stay away from motion pictures which are offensive to truth and to Christian morality. The most efficacious manner of obtaining these pledges or promises is through the parish church or school" (Pius XI, Encyclical Letter, *Vigilanti Cura, On the Motion Pictures*).

"The proper and immediate end of Christian education is to cooperate with divine grace in forming the true and perfect Christian, that is, to form Christ Himself in those regenerated by Baptism. . . For the true Christian must live a supernatural life in Christ. . . and display it in all his actions. . . Hence the true Christian, product of Christian education, is the supernatural man who thinks, judges and acts constantly and consistently in accordance with right reason illuminated by the supernatural light of the example and teaching of Christ; in other words, to

tion of mankind. . . This is an obligation which binds not only the Bishops but also the faithful and all decent men who are solicitous for the well-being and moral health of the family, of the nation, and of human society in general" (Pius XI, Encyclical Letter, *Vigilanti Cura, On the Motion Pictures*).

"And repeatedly, as occasion offered, the Supreme Pontiff has disapproved of and most strongly condemned the immodest fashions in dress which have become customary in our times, even among Catholic women and girls. These fashions are not only gravely opposed to womanly dignity and adornment but tend most unhappily both to the temporal disgrace of such women, and what is worse, to their eternal ruin and that of others as well" (*Instruction on Modesty in Women's Dress*, issued by the Sacred Congregation of the Council, 12th Jan., 1930).

"Do not think that any precaution can be great enough in keeping the young from masters and schools whence the pes-

use the current term, the true and finished man of character. For, it is not every kind of consistency and firmness of conduct based on subjective principles, that makes true character, but only constancy in following the eternal principles of justice. . . " (Pius XI, Encyclical Letter, *Divini Illius Magistri, On the Christian Education of Youth*).

Widespread Ownership of Private Property

The Divine Plan for order calls for wide diffusion of ownership of property, in order to facilitate families in procuring the sufficiency of material goods required for the virtuous life of their members as human persons, and for Unions of owners and workers in Guilds or Corporations, reflecting the solidarity of the Mystical Body in economic organization.

"The law therefore should favor ownership, *and its policy should be to induce as many as possible to become owners*" (Leo XIII, Encyclical Letter, *Rerum Novarum, On the*

tilent breath of the Masonic Society is to be feared. Under your guidance, let parents, religious instructors, and priests having the care of souls, *use every opportunity*, in their Christian teaching, of warning their children and pupils of the infamous nature of these societies" (Leo XIII, Encyclical Letter, *Humanum Genus, On Freemasonry*).

Satan Enslaves Men by Attacking Private Property

Satan aims at the concentration of property in the hands of a few, either nominally in those of the State, that is, in those of the party in power, or in those of the money-manipulators. He knows that, given fallen human nature, this will lead to the subordination of men to production of material goods and to the treatment of all those not in power as mere *individuals*, not as *persons*. For this he favored Liberalism or Individualism and now favors the reaction against

(Our Lord's Program)	(Satan's Aims)

Condition of the Working Classes).

    "As in the conflict of interests and most of all in the struggle against unjust forces, a man's virtue does not always suffice to assure him his daily bread, and as the social machinery ought to be so organized as by its natural action to paralyze the efforts of the wicked, and to render accessible to every man of goodwill his legitimate share of temporal happiness, We earnestly desire that you should take an active share in organizing society for that purpose.. . . The Church has no need to disown her past; it is enough for her, with the cooperation of the real workmen of social organization, to take up again the organizations shattered by the Revolution [the Guilds] and in the same Christian spirit which inspired them, to adapt them to the new environment created by the material evolution of contemporary society, for the true friends of the people are neither revolutionaries, nor innovators, but men of tradition" (Pius X, Letter, *On the Subject of the Sillon*).

Individualism — Collectivism and Communism.

    Satan saw with pleasure the ruin of souls resulting from unbridled Individualism. "Even on Sundays and Holydays, labor shifts were given no time to attend to their essential religious duties. No one thought of building churches within convenient distances of factories or of facilitating the work of the priest. On the contrary, laicism was actively and persistently promoted, with the result that we are now reaping the fruits of the errors so often denounced by Our Predecessors and by Ourselves. It can surprise no one that the Communistic fallacy should be spreading in a world already to a large extent estranged from Christianity" (Pius XI, Encyclical Letter, *Divini Redemptoris, On Atheistic Communism*).

    "Very many employers treated their workmen as mere tools,

(Our Lord's Program)

"Agriculture is the first and most important of all arts; so it is also the first and true riches of States. . . To render onerous the conditions of the tiller of the soil tends to restrict his activities and to cripple rural industry" (Pius VII, *Motu Proprio*, Sept. 15, 1802).

"Because sociability is one of man's natural requirements and since it is legitimate to promote, by common effort, decent livelihood, it is not possible without injustice, to deny or to limit, either to the producers or to the laboring and farming classes, the free faculty of uniting in associations, by means of which they may defend their proper rights and secure the betterment of the goods of soul and body, as well as the honest comforts of life. But to unions of this kind, which in past centuries have procured immortal glory for Christianity and for the professions an untarnishable splendor, one cannot everywhere impose an identical discipline and structure, which, therefore, can be varied to meet the different temperament of

(Satan's Aims)

without any concern for the welfare of their souls, indeed without the slightest thought of higher interests. The mind shudders if we consider the frightful perils to which the morals of workers (of boys and young men particularly), the virtue of girls and women, are exposed in modern factories; if we recall how the present economic régime and, above all, the disagreeable housing conditions prove obstacles to the family tie and family life; if we remember the insuperable difficulties placed in the way of a proper observance of Holydays. . . Dead matter leaves the factory ennobled and transformed, while human beings are corrupted and degraded" (Pius XI, Encyclical Letter, *Quadragesimo Anno, On the Social Order*).

On the other hand, satan fans the flames of the Communist reaction and urges on the revolt

the people and the diverse circumstances of time. But let the unions in question draw their vital force from principles of wholesome liberty, let them take their form from the lofty rules of justice and of honesty and conforming themselves to those norms, let them act in such a manner that, in their care for the interests of their class, they violate no one's rights, let them continue to strive for harmony and respect the common weal of civil society" (Pius XII, Letter to the American Hierarchy, Nov. 1, 1939).

"If private resources do not suffice, it is the duty of the public authority to supply for the insufficient forces of individual effort, particularly in a matter which is of such importance to the common weal, namely, the maintenance of the family and married people. If families, particularly those in which there are many children, have not suitable dwellings; if the husband cannot find employment and means of livelihood; if the necessities of life cannot be purchased except at exhorbitant prices; if even the

against God, Our Loving Father. "In the beginning Communism showed itself for what it was in all its perversity; but very soon it realized that it was thus alienating the people. It has therefore changed its tactics, and strives to entice the multitudes by trickery of various forms. . . Thus, aware of the universal desire for peace, the leaders of Communism pretend to be the most zealous promoters and propagandists of the movement for world amity. Yet at the same time they stir up a class warfare which causes rivers of blood to flow, and, realizing that their system offers no internal guarantee of peace, they have recourse to unlimited armaments. . . They try perfidiously to worm their way even into professedly Catholic and religious organizations. . . See to it, Venerable Brethren, that the Faithful do not allow themselves to be

(Our Lord's Program)	(Satan's Aims)

mother of the family, to the great harm of the home, is compelled to go forth and seek a living by her own labor; if she, too, in the ordinary or even extraordinary labors of childbirth is deprived of proper food, medicine, and the assistance of a skilled physician, it is patent to all to what an extent married people may lose heart, and how home life and the observance of God's commands are rendered difficult for them; indeed, it is obvious how great a peril can arise to the public security and to the welfare and very life of civil society itself when such men are reduced to that condition of desperation that, having nothing which they fear to lose, they are emboldened to hope for chance advantage from the upheaval of the State and of established order" (Pope Pius XI, Encyclical Letter, *Casti Connubii, On Christian Marriage*).

deceived! Communism is intrinsically wrong, and no one who would save Christian civilization may give it assistance in any undertaking whatsoever" (Pius XI, Encyclical Letter, *Divini Redemptoris, On Atheistic Communism*).

"They (the Communists) carry out the *diabolical* program of wresting from the hearts of all, even of children, all religious sentiment. . . Thus we see today, what was never before seen in history, the *satanical* banners of war against God and against religion brazenly unfurled to the winds in the midst of all peoples and in all parts of the earth" (Pius XI, *Caritate Christi Compulsi, On the Troubles of Our Time*).

Christ's Monetary System is a Servant of Man

The Divine Plan for order calls for a monetary system so arranged as to

Satan's Monetary System is a Means to Enslave Man

Satan aims at a monetary system, by which human persons will be sub-

(Our Lord's Program)	(Satan's Aims)

facilitate the production and exchange of material goods in view of the virtuous life of the Members of Christ in happy families.

"The ancient workingmen's guilds were abolished in the last [18th] century, and no other organization took their place. Public institutions and the laws themselves have set aside the ancestral religion. Hence by degrees, it has come to pass that workingmen have been surrendered, all isolated and helpless, to the hard-heartedness of employers and the greed of unbridled competition. The evil has been increased by rapacious usury, which, although more than once condemned by the Church, is nevertheless under a different guise but with the like injustice, still practised by covetous and grasping men. To this must be added the uprise of powerful monopolies, controlling enterprises

ordinated to the production of material goods, and the production, distribution and exchange of material goods, will be subordinated to the making of money and the growth of power in the hands of the financiers. He is pleased that money is employed as an instrument for the elimination of the Divine Plan and for the installation of Naturalism. Satan favors birth-prevention. "And now, Venerable Brethren, We shall explain in detail the evils opposed to each of the benefits of matrimony. First consideration is due to the offspring, which many have the boldness to call the disagreeable burden of matrimony, and which, they say is to be carefully avoided by married people, not through virtuous continence (which Christian law permits in matrimony when both parties consent), but by frustrating the marriage act. Some justify this criminal abuse on the grounds that they are weary of children and wish to gratify their desires without the consequent burden.

"Others say that they

worked by contract and all branches of commerce; so that a very small number of very rich men have been able to lay upon the teeming masses of the proletariat a yoke little better than that of slavery itself" (Leo XIII, Encyclical Letter, *Rerum Novarum, On the Condition of the Working Classes*).

"It is patent that in our days not alone is wealth accumulated, but immense power and despotic economic domination are concentrated in the hands of a few. . . This domination is most powerfully exercised by those who, because they hold and control money, also govern credit and determine its allotment, for that reason supplying, so to speak, the life-blood to the entire economic body and grasping in their hands, as it were, the very soul of production, so that no one dare breathe against their will. . . At the time when the new social order was

cannot on the one hand remain continent nor on the other can they have children because of the difficulties on the part of the mother or on the part of family circumstances. But no reason, however grave, may be put forward by which anything intrinsically against nature may become conformable to nature and morally good. Since, therefore, the conjugal act is destined primarily by nature for the begetting of children, those who, in exercising it, deliberately frustrate its natural power and purpose, sin against nature and commit a deed which is shameful and intrinsically vicious. . .

"Since, therefore, openly departing from the uninterrupted Christian tradition, some recently have judged it possible to declare solemnly another doctrine regarding the question, the Catholic Church, to whom God has entrusted the defense of the integrity and purity of morals. . . raises her voice in token of her divine ambassadorship and through

(Our Lord's Program)	(Satan's Aims)

beginning, the doctrines of rationalism had already taken firm hold of large numbers, and an economic science, alien to the true moral law, had quickly arisen, whence it followed that free rein was given to human avarice" (Pius XI, Encyclical Letter, *Quadragesima Anno, On the Social Order*).

The Catholic Church condemns the sin of birth-prevention: "Within these sacred precincts (of the Christian family), children are considered not heavy burdens but sweet pledges of love: no reprehensible motive of convenience, no seeking after sterile pleasure bring about the frustration of the gift of life, nor cause to fall into disuse the sweet names of brother and sister" (Pius XII, Letter to the American Hierarchy, Nov. 1, 1939).

But the Catholic Church insists also that social organization must aid married people to fulfill their sacred obliga-

Our mouth proclaims anew: any use whatsoever of matrimony, exercised in such a way that the act is deliberately frustrated in its natural power to generate life, is an offense against the law of God and of nature, and those who indulge in such are branded with the guilt of a grave sin. . . No difficulty can arise that justifies putting aside the law of God which forbids all acts intrinsically evil" (Pius XI, Encyclical Letter, *Casti Connubii, On Christian Marriage*).

"The poorer section of the population have outrun the demand for manual labor. . . they must learn to regulate the expansion of their families as the middle and upper classes have long been doing" (Letter to the London Times quoted by Jeffrey Mark, in *The Modern Idolatry*, p. 35).

"Houses for slum dwellers in England cannot be built because the working classes do not have enough *money* to pay the interest and redemption charges on the loans which are needed to build them. Recent proposals for build-

(Our Lord's Program)	(Satan's Aims)

tions. "Since it is no rare thing to find that the perfect observance of God's commands and conjugal integrity encounter difficulties by reason of the fact that the husband and wife are in straitened circumstances, their necessities must be relieved as far as possible. And, in the first place, every effort must be made to bring about that which Our Predecessor, Leo XIII of happy memory, has already insisted upon, namely, that in the State such economic and social methods should be adopted as will enable every head of a family, to earn as much as, according to his station in life, is necessary for himself, his wife, and for the rearing of his children, for the 'laborer is worthy of his hire' (St. Luke, X, 7). 'To deny this or to make light of what is equitable is a grave injustice and is placed among the greatest sins by Holy Writ' (Deut. XXIV, 14, 15); nor is it

ing such houses at $£330 each would involve a rental of something between six and seven shillings a week to pay the interest and provide for repayment of the loan. If the cost were more, the rent could not be paid; if it were less, the houses would probably collapse on the occupants. . . The houses will be guaranteed not to collapse on the occupants for at least as long as the period required for the redemption of the loan" (*The Modern Idolatry*, by Jeffrey Mark, p. 39, published in 1934).

"We are sorry to note that not infrequently nowadays it happens that through a certain inversion of the true order of things, ready and bountiful assistance is provided for the unmarried mother and her illegitimate offspring (who, of course, must be helped in order to avoid a greater evil), which is denied to legitimate mothers or given sparingly or almost grudgingly.

"It is the concern of the public authority to make proper provision for matrimony and the family,

| (Our Lord's Program) | (Satan's Aims) |

lawful to fix such a scanty wage as will be insufficient for the upkeep of the family in the circumstances in which it is placed.

"Care, however, must be taken that the parties themselves, for a considerable time before entering upon the married life, should strive to dispose of or at least to diminish the material obstacles in their way. . . Provision must be made also, in the case of those who are not self-supporting, for joint aid by private or public guilds" (Pius XI, Encyclical Letter, *Casti Connubii, On Christian Marriage*).

not only in regard to temporal goods but also in other things which concern the good of souls. Just laws must be made for the protection of chastity. . . The prosperity of the State and the temporal happiness of its citizens cannot remain safe and sound where the foundation on which they are established, which is the moral order, is weakened and where the very fountain-head from which the State draws its life, namely, wedlock and the family, is obstructed by the vices of its citizens" (Pope Pius XI, Encyclical Letter, *Casti Connubii, On Christian Marriage*).

The Role of Supernatural Grace in the Public Life of Society

Our Lord Jesus Christ wants all His Members to grasp the program for order laid down by His Father and unite with Himself in the central act of submission to the Blessed Trinity, the Holy Mass. In this sacrifice the re-presentation of Calvary, all Catholics profess

Satan's Plans to Cultivate Hatred for the Supernatural Life

Satan wants to confuse and bewilder human beings, so that they may give up the idea that there is an order laid down by God, which they are bound to find out, if they do not know it already, and observe. On account of his relentless hatred of the Supernatural Life, he detests above all the central act of

their willingness to respect God's Rights and their readiness to strive, as a united body, to mold society in accordance with Our Lord's Program for Order.

"When an organism decays and becomes corrupt, it is because it has ceased to be under the action of the causes which had given it its form and constitution. To make it healthy and flourishing again, it is clearly necessary to bring it again under the vivifying action of those same causes. Now, modern society, in its foolhardy effort to escape from God, has rejected the supernatural order and divine revelation. It is thus withdrawn from the salutary efficacy of Christianity which is manifestly the most solid guarantee of order, the strongest bond of fraternity, and the inexhaustible source of all virtue, public and private. From this sacrilegious divorce has sprung the trouble which now disturbs the world. Hence modern society, which

submission to the Blessed Trinity, the Holy Sacrifice of the Mass. He strives to eliminate it wherever he can, and, where he cannot do so, he endeavors to have it treated as a mere formality not intended to influence life. He tries to get the young and inexperienced to accept that they are on the road to happiness, when they neglect the Mass and its significance for life, cast off moral restraint and reject the claims of duty.

On account of his hatred of the Supernatural Life of Grace, Satan has steadily striven to get every country that once acknowledged the essential or *per se* order of the world to reject that order and revolt against it. He considers that he has made a notable advance towards his goal when he has suceeded in having other religions placed on the same level as the True Church of Christ. *He is well aware of the anti-supernatural influence of that official attitude on the average member of society.* He knows well that "when error has become incarnate in legal formulæ and in administrative practice, it

(Our Lord's Program)	(Satan's Aims)

has gone sadly astray, must re-enter the bosom of the Church, if it wishes to secure its salvation and enjoy peace and prosperity. "Just as Christianity cannot penetrate into a soul without making it better, so it cannot enter into the public life of a people without establishing order. . . If Christianity transformed pagan society. . . so, after the terrible upheavals which unbelief has brought about in the world, it will be able to put that world again on the right road and bring back to order the states and peoples of modern times. That, however, is not all. The return of Christianity will not be a complete and efficacious remedy, if it does not mean the return to and the sincere love of the One, Holy, Catholic and Apostolic Church. Christianity is incarnate in the Catholic Church. It is identified with that perfect, Supernatural Society, sovereign in its own sphere, which is the Mystical Body of Jesus

penetrates so deeply into people's minds that it is impossible to eradicate it" (*The Kingship of Christ according to Cardinal Pie of Poitiers*, p.52).

The decay of the ideas of membership of Christ and of solidarity with Christ in the Mass, of which the Guilds of the Middle Ages were the embodiment in economic life, has proved disastrous for human personality. The attempts to remedy the evils that have arisen as a result of modern disorders do not go to the root of the evil. Power is steadily passing into the hands of the few.

G. K. Chesterton has well depicted some of the results of Satan's triumphs in economic organization. "The modern world began with the problem of the grocer and the grocer's assistant. It is in fact ending with a vast growth of grocers' assistants and no grocer. It must still be emphasized, obvious as it is, that the grocers' assistants have not *grown* into grocers. They have all remained assistants; only instead of assisting a humble human grocer, with a soul to be saved, they are

Christ and which has for Visible Head the Roman Pontiff, Successor of the Prince of the Apostles" (Leo XIII, Encyclical Letter, *Parvenu a la 25ième année*).

In the text from the Encyclical Letter, *Immortale Dei, On The Christian Constitution of States*, quoted on pages 228 and 232, we have seen that Pope Leo XIII insists primarily on the Rights of God. The essential (or *per se*) order of the world, the order which God wants, demands the acknowledgement of these Rights. Hence "we are bound absolutely to worship God in that way which He has shown to be His will" and "the Church deems it unlawful to place the various forms of divine worship on the same footing as the True Religion".

He then mentions what is secondary and accidental (*per accidens*). "The Church does not," he says, "condemn those rulers who, for the sake of securing some great good or of

assisting the International Stores or the Universal Provision Department. In other words, the servants have not become masters. They remain servants: only they are like those slaves that were held to public service in pagan antiquity; they have personal servants over them, but only an impersonal master over all. Now very broadly, one idea in the Guild is that the grocer's assistant should grow into a grocer. For that purpose, it is obviously necessary to preserve a large number of equal and independent grocers. It is necessary to prevent these grocers from being bought out or sold up by the stores or the Super-Grocer. With this object the Guild deliberately checked certain forms of competition, protected the weaker brethren. . .

"Chaucer mentions several Master craftsmen, evidently attached to a Guild, as going on his Canterbury Pilgrimage; he mentions, for instance, a Dyer and a worker in tapestry. If we compare the first with the huge development of the modern Dye Industry, we shall recognize

256

(Our Lord's Program)　　(Satan's Aims)

(Our Lord's Program)

hindering some great evil, patiently allow custom or usage to be a sort of sanction for each kind of religion having its place in the State." Then towards the end of the same Encyclical, he urges all Catholics to work for this return to order. "First and foremost it is the duty of all Catholics worthy of the name and wishful to be known as most loving children of the Church. . . to endeavour to bring back all civil society to the pattern and form of Christianity We have described."

"The law of Christ ought to hold sway in human society, and in communities, so as to be the teacher and guide of public as well as of private life. This being divinely appointed and provided, no one may resist with impunity, and it fares ill with any commonwealth in which Christian institutions are not allowed their proper place. . . The law of Christ is always to be sought from the Church, and therefore, as Christ is

(Satan's Aims)

at once the main distinction I mean. More and more people may have come to work in dye factories; more and more processes may have been invented. . . And although for some time the logic of Capitalism produced worse and worse conditions, the wisdom of Capitalists (following on the courage of Trades Unionists) may now produce (or pretend to produce) better and better conditions. But they produce better and better conditions for servants; they do not attempt to produce a Guild, which is a fraternity of masters. . .

"There rode in the cavalcade in Canterbury, along with the Dyer, the more conspicuous figure of the Doctor. . . The Doctor still exists as a roughly recognizable figure. The Dyer has totally disappeared. . . The reason why the Doctor is recognizable, and the Dyer unrecognizable is perfectly simple. It is that the Doctors not only were, but still are, organized on the idea of a Medieval Guild. . . The British Medical Council, which is the Council of a Guild. . . does what a

for men the Way, so likewise the Church is the Way, He in Himself and by His proper nature, she by His commission and by a share in His power. . .

"The security of the State demands that it should be brought back to Him from whom it ought never to have departed, to Him who is the Way, the Truth, and the Life, not for individuals only but for human society as a whole.

"Christ Our Lord must be reinstated as the Ruler of human society. It belongs to Him as do all its members. All the elements of the commonwealth: legal commands and prohibitions, popular institutions, schools, marriage, home-life, the workshop and the palace, all must be made to come to that fountain and imbibe the life that comes from Him" (Pope Leo XIII, Encyclical Letter, *Tametsi, On Christ Our Redeemer*).

Thus there will be peace on earth for men of good will and the happiness that can be ours on

Guild was supposed to do. It keeps the doctors going; it keeps the doctors alive; and it does prevent one popular quack from eating all his brethren out of house and home. It sets limits to competition; it prevents the growth of monopoly. It does not allow a fashionable physician in Harley Street to destroy the livelihood of four general practitioners in Hoxton. It does not permit one professional man to buy up all the practices, as one grocer can buy up all the grocers' shops. . . The Guild principle has in fact saved the doctor. . . as a separate social figure. . . But it is the tendency of all the separate social figures, falling into modern monopolist and impersonal tendencies, to disappear altogether. Standardization lowers the standard of personality and independence in all the types and trades" (*Chaucer*, by G.K. Chesterton, pp. 70-75). This remnant of the Guild idea is now being threatened with extinction by centralized financial control through compulsory Health Insurance, etc.

Satan ever seeks to

(Our Lord's Program)	(Satan's Aims)
our way to full union with the Blessed Trinity in Heaven.	separate men from Christ and lead them on to the hatred of God, Our Father, and so to despair. He urges to revolt against the order of the world and, when the inevitable disillusionment comes, he suggests that there is no order and that all is hopeless.
Our Lord ever seeks to unite men in love of His Father.	

This Section IV was compiled by Father Denis Fahey, C.S.Sp. a brilliant Irish professor of Theology who died in the 1950's. This outline is but a sample of his great works on the social reign of Jesus Christ. In the 50's abortion in the West was not the problem it is today. No doubt if he were alive today he would have added a section on abortion and Euthanasia. It might have read something like this:

Right To Life

(Our Lord's Program)

God, as the Creator of mankind, is the Author of human life. As such human life is sacred, God reserves to Himself the time when He Himself will take that human soul into eternity. No one, not mother, relative, court, doctor or legislator has the right to take away innocent human life, either by abortion or by euthanasia. In fact God has imposed on all legislators the positive obligation to defend the unborn by appropriate laws and sanctions. They cannot opt out of this duty to do all they can to pass these laws defending the innocent and defenceless.

(Satan's Aims)

Innocent human life can be taken away by human courts and laws. Satan wants human life not to be respected but rather killed whenever the opportunity presents itself. Jesus said: "The devil is a murderer and a liar from the beginning."

Satan particularly wants abortion so that he can rob from God these souls of the babies who die in original sin, and therefore cannot go to Heaven. Abortion was first legalized in the 20th century by Communist Russia in the 1920's and voted into Parliament in the 1960's by British Masonry.

The Rosary

"If our age in its pride laughs at and rejects Our Lady's Rosary, a countless legion of the most saintly men of every age and of every condition have not only held it most dear and have most piously recited it but have also used it at all times as a most powerful weapon to overcome the devil, to preserve the purity of their lives, to acquire virtue more zealously, in a word, to promote peace among men" (Pius XI, Encyclical Letter, Ingravescentibus Malis, On the Holy Rosary of the Blessed Virgin.

Section V

Bibliographies

Section I Short Bibliography

America:
None Dare Call It Conspiracy, Gary Allen,
Concord Press, Seal Beach, California.
Nine Men Against America, Rosalie M. Gordon,
Western Islands, Belmont, Massachusetts.
Will America Surrender? Slobodan M. Draskovich,
Devin-Adair, Old Greenwich, Connecticut.
The Lattimore Story, John T. Flynn, Devin-Adair,
Old Greenwich, Connecticut.
The Roosevelt Myth, John T. Flynn, Devin-Adair,
Old Greenwich, Connecticut.
National Suicide: Military Aid to the Soviet Union,
Anthony C. Sutton, Arlington House,
New Rochelle, New York.

Communism:
Biographical Dictionary of the Left, Francis X. Gannon,
Western Islands, Belmont, Massachusetts.
"We Will Bury You", ed. Brian Crozier, Tom Stacey Ltd,
London, England.
The Assault on the West, Ian Greig, Foreign Affairs
Publishing Co. Ltd., Petersham, Surrey, England.
*Western Technology and Soviet Economic Develop-
ment*, Antony C. Sutton, Hoover Institution Press, Stan-
ford, California.
The Rulers of Russia, Rev. Denis Fahey, Regina Publi-
cations, Dublin, Ireland.
You Can Trust the Communists (to be Communists),
Fred Schwarz, Christian Anti-Communism Crusade,
Long Beach, California.

Solzhenitsyn at Harvard, Ethics and Public Policy Centre, Washington, D.C.

Operation Keelhaul: The Story of Forced Repatriation *from 1944 to the Present*, Devin-Adair, Old Greenwich, Connecticut.

I Was a Slave in Russia, John Noble, Devin-Adair, Old Greenwich, Connecticut.

Communism, Conspiracy and Treason, KRP Publications, London, England.

The Fabian Socialist Contribution to the Communist Advance, Eric D. Butler, Australia League of Rights, Melbourne.

Germany and Japan:

Wall Street and the Rise of Hitler, Antony C. Sutton, Bloomfield Books, Sudbury, Suffolk, England.

"Oil, Deviance and the Traditional World Order Japanese and German Strategies for Violent *Change 1931-1941"*, John M. W. Chapman, Chap. 19 in *Tradition and Modern Japan*, Paul Norbury Publications, Tenterden, Kent, England.

France The Tragic Years, Sisley Huddleston, Western Islands, Belmont, Massachusetts.

United Nations:

The United Nations Conspiracy, Robert W. Lee, Western Islands, Belmont, Massachusetts.

Red Spies in the UN, Pierre J. Huss and George Carpozi, Coward-McCann, New York.

The Fearful Master: A Second Look at the UN, G. Edward Griffin, Western Islands, Belmont, Massachusetts.

Manacles for Mankind, Mark Ewell, Britons Publishing
Co., London.

Christianity:

The Workers' Charter, Pope Leo XIII, Catholic Truth
Society, London, England.
The Social Order, Pope Pius XI, Catholic Truth Society,
London, England.
Atheistic Communism, Pope Pius XI, Catholic Truth
Society, London, England.
Marriage and the Moral Law, Pope Pius XII,
Catholic Truth Society, London, England.
The Kingship of Christ and Organized Naturalism,
Rev. Denis Fahey, Regina Publications,
Dublin, Ireland.
The Mystical Body of Christ in the Modern World,
Rev. Denis Fahey, Regina Publications,
Dublin, Ireland.
*A History of the Protestant Reformation in England and
Ireland*, William Cobbett, London, England (1854-5).

Economics:

Money, A. O'Rahilly, Cork University Press, Ireland.
Social Dynamics, Eric D. Butler, Australian League of
Right, Melbourne.
Money, Manipulation and Social Order, Rev. Denis
Fahey, Regina Publications, Dublin.
Wealth, Virtual Wealth and Debt, Frederick Soddy,
Omni Publications, Hawthorne, California.
Dividing the Wealth: Are You Getting Your Share?,
Howard E. Kershner, Devin-Adair,
Old Greenwich, Connecticut.

*Foundations and Tax-Free Cash,*Gary Allen and Harold Lord Varney, American Opinion, Belmont, Massachusetts.

The Anti-Capitalistic Mentality, Ludwig von Mises, Libertarian Press, South Holland, Illinois.

Elements of Social Credit, Social Credit Secretariat, Liverpool, England (1946).

Economic Democracy, C.H. Douglas, Omni Publications, Hawthorne, California.

Miscellaneous:

You're Next on the List, David O. Woodbury, Western Islands, Belmont, Massachusetts.

The Whole of their Lives, Benjamin Gitlow, Western Islands, Belmont, Massachusetts.

Waters Flowing East, Elizabeth Fry, Britons Publishing Co.

The Federal Reserve Bank, H.S. Kenan, The Noontide Press, Los Angeles, California.

Tortured for Christ, Richard Wurmbrand, Hodder & Stoughton, London.

Sections II And III Short Bibliography

Father Nicholas Gruner S.T.L.; S.T.D. (Cand.)
World Enslavement or Peace . . . It's Up To The Pope,
Immaculate Heart Publications, 1988, 640 pages.

Father Joseph de St. Marie O.C.D.
Theological Reflections, on the act of Consecration of
the World by Pope John Paul II in Fatima. Marianum
Ephemerides Mariologiae. Rome, 1982, 54 pages. It is
also printed in English, 1983, 36 pages.

Frère Michel de la Sainte Trinité
The Whole Truth About Fatima
Vol . I   Science and The Facts, 1989, 549 pages.
Vol. II   The Secret and The Church, 1989, 850 pages.
Vol. III The Third Secret, 1990, 874 pages.
Immaculate Heart Publications.

Frère François de Marie des Anges
Fatima: The Astonishing Truth, 1993, 207 pages.
Fatima: Mary's Immaculate Heart and Your Salvation,
1993, 113 pages.

Sister Lucy of Fatima
Fatima In Lucia's Own Words, Ravengate, 1976, 200 pages.

Francis Johnson
Fatima - The Great Sign, Tan, 1980, 148 pages.

William Thomas Walsh
Our Lady of Fatima, Doubleday, 1954, 223 pages.

> **All the books listed on this page are available
> through the publisher of this book.**

Section IV Short Bibliography

Rev. Father Denis Fahey, C.S.Sp.
The Mystical Body Of Christ In The Modern World
384 pages
The Church And Farming
The Tragedy Of James Connolly
The Kingship Of Christ According To The Principles Of St. Thomas Aquinas, 200 pages
A Brief Sketch Of My Life Work, 28 pages
The Rulers Of Russia And The Russian Farmers,
57 pages
The Mystical Body Of Christ In The Modern World
384 pages
The Rulers Of Russia, 100 pages
The Kingship Of Christ And The Conversion Of The Jewish Nation, 192 pages
Money Manipulation And Social Order, 107 pages

Rev. A. Phillippe, C.S.S.R.
The Social Rights of Our Divine Lord Jesus Christ, The King From the French of Rev. Phillipe Last Printed in 1932

Prof. Godefroid Kurth
The Workingmen's Guilds of the Middle Ages
Translation and Intro by Father Fahey 64 Pages

Appendix

No Other Peace Plan Will Work
No Other Way is There to Avoid
Nuclear Destruction

Marxism, Leninism, communism is anti-Christ. Marx taught a satanic doctrine based on hatred of God and hatred of Man. Violence is the logical result of his errors. Lenin applied this doctrine in an organized way, imposing it on Russia. Lenin in 7 years was responsible for 20 million corpses. Stalin consolidated this system of organized murder and exported it to the world. As a result Stalin is responsible for 46 million corpses in 29 years. Russian communism continues to expand and impose by force its satanic anti-God, anti-Christ, anti-Catholic system of slavery and death.

All this evil is caused by sin. All these things happened because we ignored Our Lady of Fatima.

Under Gorbachev the persecution of Catholics is worse than under Stalin - Joseph Terelya tells us. Mr. Terelya was a Soviet prisoner for 23 years between 1962 - 1987 for being a Catholic.

Only obedience to Our Lady of Fatima will stop this apocalyptic beast by converting Russia.

To wilfully ignore the plea of Our Heavenly Mother would be a serious sin. Of this, Bishop Graber of Germany has said, "Knowing that the world can be utterly destroyed by the terrible weapons of mass destruction today and knowing too that this can be averted by prayer and penance as the Most Holy Virgin reminded us at Fatima, it is my sacred obligation to utilize these twin means of salvation, prayer and penance. Neglecting them I incur guilt in the destruction of the peoples. The omission of Prayer and penance -- I say this in all seriousness -- is a crime against humanity."

> Unless the Lord build the house
> They labor in vain who build it.
> Unless the Lord guard the city
> In vain does the guard keep vigil
>
> Psalm 126

Lenin in 7 years was responsible for 20,000,000 (20 million) corpses.
Stalin in 29 years was responsible for 46,000,000 (46 million) corpses.
Mao and Communists in China were responsible for 70 million corpses.

Today communism has not changed in its practice and doctrine of hatred, violence and death. This is still true of the 1990's. Write us or phone us at 1-800-263-8160 for a recent article demonstrating that Russian Communism has not changed and that despite propaganda to the contrary Russian Communism is still following its deliberate plans to enslave the whole world in the godless hell of worldwide Communism.

Worse still will happen if:
* We do not convert
* We do not heed Our Lady of Fatima
* THEN: Entire nations will be annihilated
* Many will go to hell forever
* Whole world including U.S.A. and Canada will be enslaved by Russia

. . . Message of Fatima

List Of Countries Still Effectively
Under Atheistic Russian Control

Country	Present Day Population	EnslavedSince
Russia	218,000,000	1917
Ukraine	50,000,000	1919
Estonia	1,122,000	1940
Latvia	1,951,000	1940
Lithuania	2,957,000	1940
Albania	2,019,000	1944
Yugoslavia	22,520,000	1945
Bulgaria	8,370,000	1947
Poland	32,207,000	1947
Romania	22,460.000	1947
Czechoslovakia	14,362,000	1948
North Korea	13,100.000	1948
China	988,927,000	1949
East Germany	16,100,000	1949
Hungary	10,284,000	1949
Outer Mongolia	1,174,000	1953
Tibet	1,200.000	1953
North Vietnam	17,800,000	1954
Cuba	8,074,000	1959
Cambodia	6,557,000	1975
Laos	2,825,000	1975
South Vietnam	20,000,000	1975
Angola	8,000,000	1977
Mozambique	10,000,000	1977
Ethiopia	31,000,000	1978
South Yemen	2,000,000	1978
Afghanistan	22,000,000	1980
Nicaragua	2,820,000	1980

Total Enslaved 1,537,829,000*

Our Lady of Fatima's Peace Plan is the only insurance you have from being enslaved by Communism. Heed Her Requests Now. Read Section II. Copy and circulate the Petition page 275.

Ask for a free recent report of what is really happening in the Russian empire.

*This has not changed substantially in the 1990's since Gorbachev and Yelstin have changed places.

WILL WE OBEY OUR LADY OF FATIMA OR, DO WE WANT TO BE ENSLAVED?

Union of Soviet Socialist Republics

Between 1917 and 1931 "the Russian Communist Government carried on a systematic decimation of the Catholic Church existing within the confines of pre-Soviet Russia, destroying within a time span of a little over 13 years 5 dioceses, 681 parishes and 980 churches; in the process a total of 13 bishops, 912 priests and approximately 1,600,000 of the faithful were arrested, scattered or deported". ("The Silent Church," Gussoni and Brunello, Veritas Publishers, 1954; p. 15.)

A study made by a team of research specialists for the Judiciary Committee of the U.S. House of Representatives and released late in 1964, reported: "The fate of the Catholic Church in the USSR and countries occupied by the Russians from 1917 to 1959 shows the following: (a) the number killed: 55 bishops; 12,800 priests and monks; 2.5 million Catholic believers; (b) imprisoned or deported: 199 bishops; 32,000 priests and 10 million believers; (c) 15,700 priests were forced to abandon their priesthood and accept other jobs; and (d) 8,334 theological seminaries were dissolved; 1,600 monasteries were nationalized, 31,779 churches were closed, 400 newspapers were prohibited, and all Catholic organizations were dissolved."

This book is challenging. One cannot ignore it. Either one must accept the analysis put forward or one must demonstrate where it is wrong.

Pointers

* The Shah of Iran, in a David Frost interview, made a pointed reference to the Insiders, saying "'They' wanted to put up the price of oil. They decided to take one country out of the supply and they picked on mine."

* He added: "The head of NATO arrived one day, and gave me the day and the hour on which I was to leave my country."

* High-priced oil has caused chaos in developed countries—a flood of bankruptcies, and the chain reaction—unemployment and despair.

* Joseph Kennedy asked his son John: "Do you realise what you are doing? This year they can make you President, next year they would kill you if you dared stand in their way."

* Khrushchev was sacked rather mysteriously. Immediately before his recall from his Black Sea holiday home, David Rockefeller had spent his summer holidays in Moscow.

* Later David visited Peking giving high praise to Mao, in an article in the *New York Times*

Petition to the Holy Father

Dear Holy Father,

Please, we beg you, protect us from the horrors of Militant Atheism headquartered in Russia. Help us preserve our homes, our freedom and help us to save our souls. Consecrate **Russia** to the Immaculate Heart of Mary **now** as Our Lord requested through the Message of Fatima. We offer our prayers and sacrifices to help you achieve this purpose. God Bless you and Our Lady protect you.

Signed

_____

_____

_____

_____

_____

_____

_____

_____

_____

BP03

My Pledge to Our Lady

Dear Queen and Mother, who promised at Fatima to convert Russia and bring peace to all mankind in reparation to your Immaculate Heart for my sins and the sins of the whole world, I solemnly promise: (1) to offer up every day the sacrifices demanded by my daily duty; (2) to say part of the Rosary (five decades) daily while meditating on the Mysteries; (3) to wear the Scapular of Mount Carmel as profession of this promise and as an act of consecration to you. I shall renew this promise often, especially in moments of temptation.

Signature_____

BP03

My Pledge to Our Lady

Dear Queen and Mother, who promised at Fatima to convert Russia and bring peace to all mankind in reparation to your Immaculate Heart for my sins and the sins of the whole world, I solemnly promise: (1) to offer up every day the sacrifices demanded by my daily duty; (2) to say part of the Rosary (five decades) daily while meditating on the Mysteries; (3) to wear the Scapular of Mount Carmel as profession of this promise and as an act of consecration to you. I shall renew this promise often, especially in moments of temptation.

Signature_____

BP03

My Pledge to Our Lady

Dear Queen and Mother, who promised at Fatima to convert Russia and bring peace to all mankind in reparation to your Immaculate Heart for my sins and the sins of the whole world, I solemnly promise: (1) to offer up every day the sacrifices demanded by my daily duty; (2) to say part of the Rosary (five decades) daily while meditating on the Mysteries; (3) to wear the Scapular of Mount Carmel as profession of this promise and as an act of consecration to you. I shall renew this promise often, especially in moments of temptation.

Signature_____

BP03

My Pledge to Our Lady

Dear Queen and Mother, who promised at Fatima to convert Russia and bring peace to all mankind in reparation to your Immaculate Heart for my sins and the sins of the whole world, I solemnly promise: (1) to offer up every day the sacrifices demanded by my daily duty; (2) to say part of the Rosary (five decades) daily while meditating on the Mysteries; (3) to wear the Scapular of Mount Carmel as profession of this promise and as an act of consecration to you. I shall renew this promise often, especially in moments of temptation.

Signature_____

BP03

Fatima and the Great Conspiracy Order Form

I want to help spread the authentic Fatima Message. Please send me copies of *Fatima and the Great Conspiracy.*

Enclosed is my payment in the amount of $_____.
(Please print your name and address in easily legible BLOCK letters)

NAME_____

ADDRESS_____

CITY_____

STATE/PROV._____

ZIP/POSTAL CODE_____

Price $5.00 (U.S. FUNDS)+ 1.50 Postage and Handling

Postage charges are for North American shipping only. On overseas shipping extra charges will apply.
Please include cheque or money order payable in U.S. Funds.

ORDER FROM: *Militia of Our Immaculate Mother*

IN CANADA:
Box 602
Fort Erie, Ontario L2A 4M7

IN U.S.A.:
85 Allen Street, Suite 505
Buffalo, N.Y. 14202